# GOOD MUMS, BAD MUMS

OLUWAKEMI. O. OLA-OJO

Copyright © 2005 & 2009 by Protokos Publishers

Good Mums, Bad Mums

Copyright © 2009 by Oluwakemi O. Ola-Ojo
ISBN 978-0-9557898-1-6
2nd edition

First printed in the USA - June 2005
ISBN: 1-59781-348-6

All publishing rights belong exclusively to
Protokos Publishers

*Published by:*
Protokos Publishers
P. O. Box 48424, London, SE15 2YL
www.protokospublishers.com

*Cover design:*
Prex Nigeria Limited

*Edited by:*
Prex Nigeria Limited
prexng_2000@yahoo.com

*Book Layout by:*
Nestto Graphix
(a div. of Nestto Group, LLC, Houston, Texas, USA)

*Author's photograph by:*
Hill Stanton

Printed in United Kingdom

All rights reserved under International Copyright Law. Contents and or cover may not be reproduced in whole or in part in any form without the express written consent of the Publisher.

Unless otherwise stated, all Scripture quotations are from the King James Version of the Bible.

Please note NLT means New Living Translation and NIV means New International Version.

# Dedication

To my godly grandmothers of blessed memory, Madam Leah Ojo and Madam Comfort Aloba. To Madam Sarah Ogbede, a mother and grandmother in Israel, whose life has daily blessed me and taught me self control as a little child.

To Mrs. G. M. Ojo, for her excellent cooking and timely meals, Mrs. Eileen Weston, Mrs. Joyce Tulloch, and Lady Eniola Olubobokun, for all their encouragement and support, especially at crucial times.

To all my mentors and Pastors who have fed me over the years with the truth from the living word of God.

To my Mother, Mrs. Modupe Ojo, the best mother and teacher in the world, in whom I have seen and learnt the virtues of outstanding dedication, love and excellence.

To my biological and spiritual sisters, Foluso, Ruth, Elizabeth, and Mary Adeniyi, whose love, prayers and support, I have enjoyed all these years.

To Mosun, Imoh, Rachel, Sharon, Janet and my other friends, whose friendship has richly enhanced my life.

# Acknowledgement

THE COUNSEL OF MANY God fearing and God loving people has blessed me. Thank you all for your suggestions and corrections; they have been thankfully received. Thanks to Mrs. Bolanle Sogunro for editing this book, the management and staff of Prex Holdings for the book cover, and Protokos Publishers, for helping to get this into print.

# CONTENTS

| | | |
|---|---|---|
| Dedication | | 3 |
| Acknowledgement | | 5 |
| About This Book | | 9 |
| Chapter 1: | Trust No One<br>*Athaliah* | 15 |
| Chapter 2: | No One But Jesus<br>*Hannah* | 33 |
| Chapter 3: | Casting All Upon Him<br>*Jochebed* | 51 |
| Chapter 4: | In The Twinkle Of An Eye<br>*Rebecca* | 71 |
| Chapter 5: | God's Gift You Can Never Buy<br>*The Shunammite Woman* | 87 |
| Chapter 6: | God's Provision—My Part<br>*Unnamed Prophet's Widow* | 103 |
| Chapter 7: | Christmas Is About Willingness<br>*Mary – Mother of Jesus* | 121 |
| Chapter 8: | A Psalm For Every Mum | 145 |
| Opportunity to Become a Christian | | 149 |
| Books by the Author | | 153 |
| Useful Links & Addresses | | 161 |

# About This Book

IN THE HUMAN SPECIE, only women can biologically conceive. During the period of pregnancy, the mother contributes a lot to her baby's welfare. Her diet, habits, including alcohol consumption and drug use, the kind of music she listens to, her general well being or otherwise, all sometimes have a temporary or permanent, negative or positive effect on the unborn child.

The privileged position of a mother is in her being a co-creator with God and bringing forth children that will have dominion over all the earth: the fish of the sea, the fowl of the air, the cattle, and over every creeping thing upon the earth (Genesis 1:26). What goes into the woman is a seed of the man but what comes out of her at full term is a child. No wonder Eve said, "I have produced a man with the help of the Lord" (Genesis 4:1, NIV).

This book compliments one of God's previous revelations to me that I have shared in my book titled, *Good Dads, Bad Dads*. Using the image of air travel, a husband can be likened to the pilot of the family aeroplane while his wife is the force—positive or negative-behind the plane; complementing her husband in the upbringing and training of their children.

In an ideal home, the mother, like the woman in Proverbs 31:10–31, is hard-working and highly organized, aware of and in control of everything that goes on in her household. She is knowledgeable, thinks properly before taking investment decisions, makes adequate provision for her family, and supports her husband. She is trustworthy, wise and kind.

Good mothers are not only co-creators with God, they have to nurture, and nourish their children physically, emotionally and spiritually. Indeed theirs are the hands that rock the cradle, which invariably rules the world.

The lyrics of two well-known African songs that are dedicated to, and celebrate motherhood aptly express the invaluable input of a good mother in every child's life. The first is an old popular *Yoruba* song:

*Iya ni wura iyebiye; Ti a ko le f'owo ra,*
*Oloyun mi f'osu mesan; O pon mi f'odun mefa,*
*Iya ni wura iyebiye; Ti a ko le f'owo ra.*

The song translated literally goes thus:

*Mother is the precious gold,*
*That cannot be purchased with money.*
*She had me in her womb for nine months;*
*Bore me on her back for six years,*

## About This Book

*Mother is the precious gold;*
*That cannot be purchased with money.*

The other song is in *Pidgin* English, by Prince Nico Mbaga, goes thus:

*Sweet mother, I no go forget you,*
*For di suffer wey you suffer for me,*
*Wen I no sleep, my mother no go sleep,*
*Wen I no chop, my mother no go chop,*
*She no dey taya, sweet mother,*
*I no go forget the suffer whey you suffer for me yey, yey*
*Sweet mother, ah ha ah, sweet mother o, eh o*

Translated, it says:

*Sweet mother I will not forget you*
*For all your sufferings on my behalf*
*When I can't sleep, my mother will not sleep,*
*When I can't eat, my mother will not eat,*
*She is never tired, sweet mother,*
*I will not forget all of your sufferings on my behalf*
*Sweet mother, sweet mother.*

Unfortunately, not all mothers can be described as "sweet" or as "precious gold" and that is the reason for this book, on good and bad mothers. It is a study based on an examination of seven mothers in the Old and New Testaments of the Bible.

Why seven mothers, you might ask? Seven because that was the number the Holy Spirit gave me to write about. He also impressed on my heart which particular seven to write on, showing the impact their good and bad qualities had on their offspring. The issues relating to motherhood have not changed, and today's mother can learn a lot from the accounts of mothers like her in the Scriptures.

Thought provoking exercises are placed at the end of each character study to assist women, individual or groups, to examine their own lives, in the light of what has been presented about the life of each of these seven biblical mothers. Their strengths and weaknesses, opportunities and threats, successes, failures and so on, are examples for us to learn from. To get the best out of the exercises, you should be willing to honestly assess your personal life based on God's Word and the truths shared in this book. You should also desire to positively change and not be afraid to seek for matured Christian mentorship and counsel where necessary.

Our God always gives the repentant sinner another chance, so please don't be afraid or too proud to call upon Him. Cry, if you must, as you work through these exercises. Let the woman and mother in you cry in repentance. Cry to Jesus Christ for His salvation and healing; cry on behalf of your children and family; cry to the Holy Spirit for guidance, deliverance and wisdom.

## About This Book

As we look at the lives of these seven mothers in the Bible, my prayer is that the Lord will open your eyes to behold His marvellous, wonderful truths about good motherhood, encourage you where you are strong, challenge you where you are weak, motivate you where you are struggling and envelope you in His arms of approval, blessing, and comfort.

CHAPTER ONE

# Trust No One

HUMAN BEINGS HAVE THE tendency to put their trust in man, wealth, position, protective powers or self. What a mistake to put one's trust in either some or all of these. As none of them can save, heal, protect or provide. "Trust in your money and down you go," says the Bible. Trust in God and flourish as a tree by the riverside. Trust in your riches and be disappointed on the last day, as only faith in Christ and righteousness will count then.

Trust in yourself and you will be surprised to see that you who think you are standing will fall flat to temptation. Trust in your wealth and see it disappearing very fast as though they had the wings of an eagle to fly. Trust no man, my brother, my sister, I appeal to you. Never trust your servants, friends or relatives. As good as king Joash of Judah was in God's sight, Jozachar and Jehozabad, his servants, assassinated him.

Ben-hadad, on his sick bed sent Hazael, his servant to Elisha, to find out if he will recover from the illness. What a mishap, as Hazeal got Ben-hadad suffocated in a bid to become Israel's king as prophesied by Elisha. Some fathers sacrificed their children to idols in the Bible. Rebecca collaborated with Jacob to rob Esau of his blessing. Wicked grandma Athaliah of Judah killed all her grandsons except for Joash, who was hidden by Aunt Jehoshabeath.

Trust none of your relatives, no matter how close they are to you. Neither should you trust any of your close associates or friends too. Judas Iscariot, despite his closeness and activeness in the group, betrayed Jesus Christ just for thirty pieces of silver.

The Bible says the heart of man is desperately wicked and corrupt; who can know it except the LORD who made all mankind? A man may sound very promising, helpful, loving and kind, but his heart may be full of deadly poison, ready to kill.

"In what or in who should you then trust," you would want to ask? Not in your wealth, position, yourself, or in any other man. My brother, my sister, I admonish you to please put your total trust and hope in GOD—the only one who does not fail and will not disappoint you.

Copyright © O. Ola-Ojo 29/5/82, Based on Micah 7:5-6; Proverbs 11:28; 11:4; 23:4-5; 2 Kings 8:8-9, 19-21.

# ATHALIAH

Athaliah was a wicked queen mother, who rather than mourn the death of her son, murdered all her grandsons

# Chapter 1 - Trust No One

in order to become queen. She ended up being killed mercilessly by her subjects.

## Her Story

*Then the people of Jerusalem made Ahaziah, Jehoram's youngest son, their next king. The marauding bands of Arabs had killed all the older sons. So Ahaziah son of Jehoram reigned as king of Judah.*

*Ahaziah was twenty-two years old when he became king, and he reigned in Jerusalem one year. His mother was Athaliah, granddaughter of King Omri of Israel. Ahaziah also followed the evil example of King Ahab's family, for his mother encouraged him in doing wrong. He did what was evil in the Lord's sight, just as Ahab had done.*

*After the death of his father, members of Ahab's family became his advisers, and they led him to ruin. Following their evil advice, Ahaziah made an alliance with King Joram, the son of King Ahab of Israel. They went out to fight King Hazael of Aram at Ramoth-gilead, and the Arameans wounded Joram in the battle. Joram returned to Jezreel to recover from his wounds, and King Ahaziah of Judah went to Jezreel to visit him.*

*But this turned out to be a fatal mistake, for God had decided to punish Ahaziah. It was during this visit that Ahaziah went out with Joram to meet Jehu son of Nimshi, whom the Lord had appointed to end the dynasty of Ahab. While Jehu was executing judgment against the family of Ahab, he happened to meet some of Judah's officials and Ahaziah's relatives who were attending Ahaziah. So Jehu killed them all.*

*Then Jehu's men searched for Ahaziah, and they found him hiding in the city of Samaria. They brought him to Jehu, who killed him. Ahaziah was given a decent burial because the people said, "He was the grandson of Jehoshaphat-a man who sought the Lord with all his heart." None of the surviving members of Ahaziah's family was capable of ruling the kingdom.*

*When Athaliah, the mother of King Ahaziah of Judah, learned that her son was dead, she set out to destroy the rest of Judah's royal family. But Ahaziah's sister Jehosheba, the daughter of King Jehoram, took Ahaziah's infant son, Joash, and stole him away from among the rest of the king's children, who were about to be killed.*

*She put Joash and his nurse in a bedroom. In this way, Jehosheba, the wife of Jehoiada the priest, hid the child so that Athaliah could not murder him. Joash remained hidden in the Temple of God for six years while Athaliah ruled over the land. (2 Chronicles 22:1-12, NLT)*

*In the seventh year of Athaliah's reign, Jehoiada the priest decided to act. He got up his courage and made a pact with five army commanders: Azariah son of Jeroham, Ishmael son of Jehohanan, Azariah son of Obed, Maaseiah son of Adaiah, and Elishaphat son of Zicri. These men travelled secretly throughout Judah and summoned the Levites and clan leaders in Judah's towns to come to Jerusalem. They all gathered at the Temple of*

## Chapter 1 - Trust No One

*God, where they made a covenant with Joash, the young king. Jehoiada said to them, "The time has come for the king's son to reign! The Lord has promised that a descendant of David will be our king.*

*This is what you must do. When the priests and Levites come on duty on the Sabbath, a third of them will serve as gatekeepers. Another third will go over to the royal palace, and the final third will be at the Foundation Gate. Everyone else should stay in the courtyards of the Lord's Temple. Remember, only the priests and Levites on duty may enter the Temple of the Lord, for they are set apart as holy. The rest of the people must obey the Lord's instructions and stay outside.*

*You Levites, form a bodyguard for the king and keep your weapons in hand. Any unauthorized person who enters the Temple must be killed. Stay right beside the king at all times. "So the Levites and the people did everything just as Jehoiada the priest ordered. The commanders took charge of the men reporting for duty that Sabbath, as well as those who were going off duty. Jehoiada the priest did not let anyone go home after their shift ended.*

*Then Jehoiada supplied the commanders with the spears and shields that had once belonged to King David and were stored in the Temple of God. He stationed the guards around the king, with their weapons ready. They formed a line from the south side of the Temple around to the north side and all around the altar.*

*Then Jehoiada and his sons brought out Joash, the king's*

son, and placed the crown on his head. They presented Joash with a copy of God's laws and proclaimed him king. Then they anointed him, and everyone shouted, "Long live the king!" When Athaliah heard the noise of the people running and the shouts of praise to the king, she hurried to the Lord's Temple to see what was happening.

And she saw the newly crowned king standing in his place of authority by the pillar at the Temple entrance. The officers and trumpeters were surrounding him, and people from all over the land were rejoicing and blowing trumpets. Singers with musical instruments were leading the people in a great celebration. When Athaliah saw all this, she tore her clothes in despair and shouted, "Treason! Treason!"

Then Jehoiada the priest ordered the commanders who were in charge of the troops, "Take her out of the Temple, and kill anyone who tries to rescue her. Do not kill her here in the Temple of the Lord. "So they seized her and led her out to the gate where horses enter the palace grounds, and they killed her there. Then Jehoiada made a covenant between himself and the king and the people that they would be the Lord's people… So all the people of the land rejoiced, and the city was peaceful because Athaliah had been killed. (2 Chronicles 23:1-16, 21, NLT)

## Give Good Counsel

Athaliah was king Ahaziah's mother and counsellor. He was twenty-two years old when he began to reign in

Jerusalem. The Bible says he was a wicked king and this could be traced to the counsel he received from his mother. It is not wrong for a mother to give counsel to her son even if he is the ruling king, but the kind of advice given is important. Proverbs 31 was the good advice of a mother to her son king Lemuel. Mum, the counsel you give your children should be one that honours Christ and God's people. You need to fear God in all your endeavours, seeking to please Him alone.

## PROTECTOR TURNS PREDATOR

It is amazing that when Athaliah heard about her son's death, she did not cry or mourn; rather she did the unnatural by killing her grandchildren and all successors to the throne, and then proclaimed herself the ruling queen. What a bizarre thing to done!

A *Yoruba* proverb says, *"B'iku ile ko ba pani, t'ode ko le pani."* This means, unless you get killed (or betrayed) first from within your family or circle of friends, an outsider cannot kill you. Could it be that all the while that her son was alive, Athaliah had been planning to kill him herself? Had she been praying and making plans to succeed her son? In most cultures, even in the 21st century, the natural thing is for children to succeed their parents, and not vice versa.

Was Athaliah power-thirsty or power-drunk? Under

normal circumstances, she should have protected her grandchildren from enemies and intruders after the death of her son. These children must have been confident that though their father was dead, their grandmother will see to it that they came to no harm, but she was the very person who turned around to kill them. Athaliah reigned for at least six years, but her reign was not remarkable. If she could kill all her innocent grandchildren, who else could she not hurt or kill? She was definitely a wicked and dangerous woman.

While it is not clear why Athaliah killed all her grandchildren, and why she did not weep over her son's death, it is not uncommon in the occult world for mothers to offer their children or grandchildren for ritual sacrifice. Was Athaliah a witch? Was she in the occult or demon-possessed?

## You May Be "Killing" Your Child

Some mothers have indirectly killed their children by what they thought were simple acts, but have gone on to have lasting effects on their children. For example, uncontrolled or unchecked malnutrition can affect the mental development of a child, which in turn will affect future academic performance. This is apart from making the child more vulnerable to various childhood diseases. Mother, do you spend the family income on buying new

## Chapter 1 - Trust No One

clothing for yourself at the expense of feeding your children properly and taking good care of them?

A mother who keeps telling her child that his or her birth was an accident, an unwanted pregnancy, an added stress or burden to her busy life, may leave a permanent psychological dent on that child. A mother who leaves her daughter in the hands of a boyfriend or any other child in the custody of a nanny who is nothing, but a child molester may kill the emotions of love, affection and trust in that child, breeding in its place, feelings of fear, anger and distrust.

Some mothers constantly wish and make evil confessions about their children. The fact that you had a difficult pregnancy or gave birth in unpleasant circumstances should not make you give your child a bad name as Jabez's mother did (see 2 Chronicles 4:9-10). A child's destiny is often linked to his or her name.

Equally, you should avoid using bad words (e.g. lazy bone, silly boy, empty head, big head, naughty one, disgraceful child, etc.) to describe your child. The damaging effect cannot be quantified. It is true that, as a mother, you need to deal with wrong behaviour, but not in a way that puts your child down, or makes him or her feel less than what God created him or her to be.

Instead of sorting out their marital problems, some women take out their frustrations on their children by cursing and physically abusing them. Punishing children on account of their father or any other family member is very unfair and usually has a damaging effect on them.

What about the racist mother who brings up her children to be the same? She is as bad as mothers who are prostitutes, shoplifters, gossipers, etc., who teach their children to walk in the same, self-destructive path they tread. Other mothers have "killed" their children by openly rejecting them for having a medical challenge, for being born a different sex from what they expected, for not looking or acting the way they expected, or simply for just not looking or acting like their siblings.

A number of adults are in frustrating careers today because their parents forced them to do courses they had no real passion for. Many others are in frustrating marriages and relationships because their mothers coerced them into it.

Their experience can be likened to living in hell here on earth all because they want to make mummy happy. Children from separated homes most often also go through a form of death in one way or the other. I know adults who suffer from periodic depression because they have not been able to overcome the social and psychological effects of their parents' separation.

A rather disturbing trend today is that of mothers who sexually abuse their children. They use their own sons or other people's sons as sex toys; destroying their innocence and youth, polluting their minds; ravaging their emotions, encouraging promiscuity; exposing them to sexually transmitted diseases; mortgaging the future relationships of the poor boys.

## SUBTLE INITIATION

It is sad that many mothers, unfortunately Christians inclusive, have ignorantly enrolled their children in occult practice. How? By not checking things out before joining the "Joneses". They buy games and films that invariably destroy their children. I once heard an American Preacher share the testimony of a young girl whose deliverance he was involved in. Her parents referred her to the pastor because of a sudden change in her character and demeanour.

As he prayed for her, the girl started manifesting some demonic behaviour. Eventually, he found out that the sudden change started after the young girl went to watch a particular film. The demon in the girl confirmed entering into her at the cinema.

Mother what are you exposing your child to? What do you allow your children to watch or participate in? Who is looking after those children when you travel or are at work? Who is feeding them what? Or are you one of those mothers who have physically destroyed their children, or other person's, by willing them to a secret society or cult? If you are, then the blood of those whose lives you have terminated prematurely is upon your head and you can be sure of a disgraceful, merciless end like that of Athaliah.

Are you a kind or a wicked mother? Are you a protector or destroyer of life? Are you one of those mothers who stir up trouble among their children using the tactic of divide and rule? An Athaliah-like mum will not mind who gets hurt or destroyed for her to satisfy her ungodly desire or unholy ambition, not even her own offspring. May the good Lord deliver us from such mothers in Jesus name.

God is watching over all of your actions and you will be judged for whatever you do to the precious lives in your care. However if you confess your sins and repent before the Lord and decide to live a new life, there is hope for you. Please, if anything, don't be like Athaliah the wicked mother and grandmother.

Come just as you are to Jesus Christ, confessing all your sins including your wicked acts. He will forgive you of them all and cleanse you from every form of unrighteousness. He who gave a second chance to Moses the murderer, Saul the persecutor, and Peter the betrayer is willing to help you too as you get back to Him in total obedience. God is willing and able to give you a fresh start so that you do not need to continue in your line of sin and fear.

Take time now to read the following scriptures in the

Bible: 1John 1:8-9, John 3:16-17, Isaiah 1:11-20. God is the God of new beginnings. In Him you can live a new, purposeful, rewarding, God glorifying, people oriented and blessed life.

## EXERCISE ONE:

**Evaluate your life from Athaliah's story...**

**A.**

1. Athaliah gave a wicked counsel to her son the king. Examine what sort of counsel you are giving to your children and why?

2. In what ways can the weakness or wickedness in your children be traced to you?

3. Repent and ask God to help you to correct them.

**B.**

1. In raising your children, have you done any unthinkable thing to any of them? If so, why?

2. In what ways have you "killed" your child(ren) or grandchildren or other people's children and why?

3. In what ways have you taken over any of your children's family or property, especially what belongs to that child that is no more?

4. Repent of this and return such property to the rightful owners—your in-laws, your grand child(ren), etc.

## C.

1. Are you a kind or wicked mother? List at least three reasons you think would make your children call you either kind or wicked.

    a.
    b.
    c.

2. Do you find it easier to be a protector of life or a destroyer of it?

3. Are you one of the mothers who stir up trouble in their family especially among their children using the tactic of divide and rule? If so why?

4. In what ways have you willed your child(ren) to death in the secret society/cult that you have joined?

5. In what ways have you ruined your child(ren) by your attitude, spoken words, actions etc.? Repent of these and be reconciled with the child(ren) if possible.

6. Are you in any secret cult and you wish to come out clean of it now?

If yes, you will need to talk and pray it through with a mature Christian counsellor. Don't die a shameful death but turn to the Lord now and come out clean. You can take the first step by saying this prayer out loud and meaning every word of it:

*Heavenly Father, I have joined the occult group looking for powers contrary to Your power. Lord, I have done many wicked acts and now I repent of them all. Please Jesus, I confess the following wicked acts of mine (please list them), and I ask for Your mercy, Your cleansing by the power that is in the blood of Jesus, and for Your matchless grace to move on from now only in Your name and Your will.*

## Chapter 1 - Trust No One

If you have not found yourself absolutely perfect and free of any act of wickedness no matter how subtle, then please say this prayer out loud:

*Dear FATHER, In the name of Jesus Christ, I come to you just as I am. I thank You, Lord for the opportunity of reading this book. In many ways my life has been like that of Athaliah (you might wish to mention them), I have done wicked acts including (you might wish to list them), but now I confess them all to You and repent of them all.*

## Prayer For Help

*Of a truth Lord, I have fallen short of being a godly mother. FATHER, I come to You confessing all my wicked acts <u>including</u> gossiping and backbiting. With my words and actions I have not shown love to my children and I have selfishly counselled them to favour my want and wishes. Please forgive me. I thank You for Your cleansing and my forgiveness according to 1 John 1:8-9. I need Your help to live a Godly life, to read Your Word, understand it, obey it, teach and live by it in Jesus' name.*

*I need Your help in bringing up and counselling our children in the love and fear of the Lord so that each one of them will live by Your word not by the standard of the world even when we as parents are not there to see what is going on. In Jesus name I have prayed and with thanksgiving. Amen.*

CHAPTER TWO
# No One But Jesus

*No one but JESUS knows my pains*
*No one but JESUS knows my thoughts*
*No one but JESUS knows my sins*
*No one but JESUS knows my strengths.*

*Chorus:*
*No, no one **but** JESUS (or **like**)*
*No, no one but JESUS*
*No, no one but JESUS*
*No, no one but JESUS*

*No one but JESUS can heal my disease*
*No one but JESUS can take care of me*
*No one but JESUS can bless me indeed*
*No one but JESUS can make me whole.*

*No one but JESUS can fill an empty heart*
*No one but JESUS can feed a lonely soul*
*No one but JESUS can save a sinful soul*
*No one but JESUS can fill an empty womb.*

*No one but JESUS can see me through my struggles*
*No one but JESUS can see me through my trials*
*No one but JESUS can see me through my temptations*
*No one but JESUS can see me through my wilderness.*

*No one but JESUS can allay my fears*
*No one but JESUS can comfort in / sorrow*
*No one but JESUS can strengthen the weak*
*No one but JESUS can encourage the weary.*

*No one but JESUS can strengthen my tired feet*
*No one but JESUS can motivate my weary soul*
*No one but JESUS can hold my weak hands*
*No one but JESUS can touch my painful body.*
*No one but JESUS can keep me together in one piece*

*Copyright © O. Ola-Ojo 05/06/03*

# HANNAH

Hannah was an intercessor whose barrenness was changed by God to fruitfulness after she poured out her soul to Him in prayer. She vowed the first fruit of her womb to God and faithfully kept her promise.

## Her Story

*There was a man named Elkanah who lived in Ramah in the hill country of Ephraim. He was the son of Jeroham and*

## Chapter 2 - No One But Jesus

*grandson of Elihu, from the family of Tohu and the clan of Zuph. Elkanah had two wives, Hannah and Peninnah. Peninnah had children, while Hannah did not. Each year Elkanah and his family would travel to Shiloh to worship and sacrifice to the Lord Almighty at the Tabernacle. The priests of the Lord at that time were the two sons of Eli-Hophni and Phinehas.*

*On the day Elkanah presented his sacrifice, he would give portions of the sacrifice to Peninnah and each of her children. But he gave Hannah a special portion because he loved her very much, even though the Lord had given her no children. But Peninnah made fun of Hannah because the Lord had closed her womb. Year after year it was the same-Peninnah would taunt Hannah as they went to the Tabernacle. Hannah would finally be reduced to tears and would not even eat.*

*"What's the matter, Hannah?" Elkanah would ask. "Why aren't you eating? Why be so sad just because you have no children? You have me-isn't that better than having ten sons?" Once when they were at Shiloh, Hannah went over to the Tabernacle after supper to pray to the Lord. Eli the priest was sitting at his customary place beside the entrance. Hannah was in deep anguish, crying bitterly as she prayed to the Lord.*

*And she made this vow: "O Lord Almighty, if you will look down upon my sorrow and answer my prayer and give me a son, then I will give him back to you. He will be yours for his entire lifetime, and as a sign that he has been dedicated to the Lord, his hair will never be cut." As she was praying to the Lord, Eli* watched her. Seeing her lips moving but hearing no sound, he thought she had been drinking.

"Must you come here drunk?" he demanded. "Throw away your wine!" "Oh no, sir!" she replied, "I'm not drunk! But I am very sad, and I was pouring out my heart to the Lord. Please don't think I am a wicked woman! For I have been praying out of great anguish and sorrow." "In that case," Eli said, "cheer up! May the God of Israel grant the request you have asked of him." "Oh, thank you, sir!" she exclaimed. Then she went back and began to eat again, and she was no longer sad.

The entire family got up early the next morning and went to worship the Lord once more. Then they returned home to Ramah. When Elkanah slept with Hannah, the Lord remembered her request, and in due time she gave birth to a son. She named him Samuel, for she said, "I asked the Lord for him."

The next year Elkanah, Peninnah, and their children went on their annual trip to offer a sacrifice to the Lord. But Hannah did not go. She told her husband, "Wait until the baby is weaned. Then I will take him to the Tabernacle and leave him there with the Lord permanently." "Whatever you think is best," Elkanah agreed. "Stay here for now, and may the Lord help you keep your promise." So she stayed home and nursed the baby. When the child was weaned, Hannah took him to the Tabernacle in Shiloh. They brought along a three-year-old bull for the sacrifice and half a bushel of flour and some wine.

After sacrificing the bull, they took the child to Eli. "Sir, do *you remember me?" Hannah asked. "I am the woman who stood here several years ago praying to the Lord. I asked the Lord to give me this child, and he has given me my request. Now I am giving him to the Lord, and he will belong to the Lord his whole life." And they worshipped the Lord there. (1 Samuel 1:1-end, NLT)*

## THE PAIN OF INFERTILITY

Those who have never experienced barrenness cannot comprehend the pain of infertility or sub fertility and so they are sometimes insensitive to the anguish experienced by those affected. The society is woven around the family and often it may be difficult for a childless couple to attend family celebrations as they are often deliberately or inadvertently reminded of their infertility, by insensitive comments or acts. It is ungodly and wicked to mock childless women. It is also ignorance that makes one think that barrenness, infertility or sub fertility in a person or couple is a result of sin.

In Hannah's case it was the Lord who deliberately closed her womb! Hannah was the first of the two wives of Elkanah. Although much loved by her husband, her fruitful mate's taunting and mockery always kept her dejected. Nothing her husband did could make up for Hannah's childlessness or Penninah's cruel remarks (1 Samuel 1:4-8). A high level of anxiety and emotional distress is often seen especially in the partner whose fruitfulness is being questioned in infertility.

## Don't Give Up Yet!

For Hannah, it was a time of sorrow, shame and reproach yet she continued to make the yearly trip to Shiloh even though her prayers seemed unanswered (1 Samuel 1:3) Some people today have stopped praying, singing, and fellowshipping with others in the Church due to frustration, bitterness, unforgiveness, insensitivity or total lack of faith in God. Loyalty and obedience to God must be constant, no matter the situation.

Your attitude should be like that of Job who said ...*all the days of my appointed time will I wait until my change come* (Job 14:14). Sister, what is it that you have been asking or trusting God for? Don't give up yet; keep coming into the house of the Lord irrespective of mockers like Peninnah around you.

## Tell It To Jesus

One day at Shiloh, Hannah made up her mind to visit the temple by herself and talk to God privately. She prayed intensely, moving her lips but not uttering a word: the prophet assumed she was drunk. Hannah took charge of her life, entrusting it into the Lord's hands. What is causing you grief sister? It is high time you make up your mind about it and present it to the Lord. You need to open the reservoir of your heart in prayers and tell your hurt as it is to Jesus just as the song says:

*Are you weary, are you heavy hearted?*
*Tell it to Jesus tell it to Jesus.*
*Are you grieving over joys departed?*
*Tell it to Jesus alone.*

*Refrain:*
*Tell it to Jesus tell it to Jesus,*
*He is a friend that's well known.*
*You've no other such a friend or brother,*
*Tell it to Jesus alone.*

*Do the tears flow down your cheeks unbidden?*
*Tell it to Jesus tell it to Jesus.*
*Have you sins that to men's eyes are hidden?*
*Tell it to Jesus alone.*

*Do you fear the gathering clouds of sorrow?*
*Tell it to Jesus tell it to Jesus.*
*Are you anxious what shall be tomorrow?*
*Tell it to Jesus alone.*

*Are you troubled at the thought of dying?*
*Tell it to Jesus tell it to Jesus.*
*For Christ's coming kingdom are you sighing?*
*Tell it to Jesus alone.*

Words: Edmund S. Lorenz, in *Fröliche Botschafter*, 1876, translated from German to English by Jeremiah E. Rankin in *Gates of Praise*, 1880. Source: http://cyberhymnal.org

Many who do not know what you are going through may, misjudge you like Eli did when he saw Hannah praying; others may mistreat you but refuse to be moved or aggrieved by them. Hannah's prayer was specific, not lengthy and was targeted at her greatest need. Stay focused in your prayers and relationship with the Lord Jesus Christ for only such connections come quickly to the Master's attention and gain approval (See Mark 10:46-50; Luke 18:35-48).

## God Will Remember You

We serve the God of miracles who hears loud as well as silent prayers so long as they are focused. Elkanah could not fully appreciate Hannah's plight and so did not have a separate intercession for her like Abraham, Isaac and Jacob did when their own wives suffered infertility. All the same Hannah believed and acted on the words of Prophet Eli as she allowed her husband to continue to make love to her. And the Lord remembered her (1Samuel 1:19).

Hannah got her first child through personal intercession not through strife, fighting, anger, jealousy, backbiting and so on. Sister, God is no respecter of persons but He is committed to anyone who has faith in Him. You will be remembered as He remembered Hannah. He will turn your misery into a miracle, your mourning into dancing, and your ridicule into rejoicing if only you have faith.

## Good Mum's Acknowledge God

Hannah was a promise keeper. She acknowledged that her son was a gift from God and named him Samuel, meaning "because I have asked him of the Lord." As soon as her first son (and only child then) was weaned, she gave him to the Lord to minister in His temple as she had promised. With her husband's consent, she took Samuel to live with Eli the high priest at Shiloh.

With joy in her heart, Hannah offered her son to the Lord, and rendered one of the most wonderful songs in the Bible:

*"My heart rejoices in the Lord! Oh, how the Lord has blessed me! Now I have an answer for my enemies, as I delight in your deliverance. No one is holy like the Lord! There is no one besides you; there is no Rock like our God.*

*"Stop acting so proud and haughty! Don't speak with such arrogance! The Lord is a God who knows your deeds; and he will judge you for what you have done. Those who were mighty are mighty no more; and those who were weak are now strong. Those who were well fed are now starving; and those who were starving are now full. The barren woman now has seven children; but the woman with many children will have no more.*

"The Lord brings both death and life; he brings some down to the grave but raises others up. The Lord makes one poor and another rich; he brings one down and lifts another up. He lifts the poor from the dust—yes, from a pile of ashes! He treats them like princes, placing them in seats of honor. For all the earth is the Lord's, and he has set the world in order.

"He will protect his godly ones, but the wicked will perish in darkness. No one will succeed by strength alone. Those who fight against the Lord will be broken. He thunders against them from heaven; the Lord judges throughout the earth. He gives mighty strength to his king; he increases the might of his anointed one" (1Samuel 2:1-10, NLT).

Hannah continued going to Shiloh to worship annually even after giving the first fruit of her womb to the Lord. She remained a loving, caring and faithful mother to Samuel, making him outfits, which she took with her to Shiloh every year. The words of Psalm 126 verses 1 to 6 best describe the joy of answered prayers and the reward of giving sacrificially to God:

*"When the Lord turned again the captivity of Zion, we were like them that dream. Then was our mouth filled with laughter, and our tongue with singing: then said they among the heathen, The Lord hath done great things for them. The Lord hath done great things for us; whereof we are glad. Turn again our captivity, O Lord, as the streams in the south. They that sow in tears shall reap in joy. He that goeth forth and weepeth, bearing precious*

## CHAPTER 2 - NO ONE BUT JESUS

*seed, shall doubtless come again with rejoicing, bringing his sheaves with him."*

Sister, that you are having difficulties conceiving or maintaining a pregnancy today does not mean you will not have children later. Our God is able to change that which seems humanly impossible. Hang in there, don't give up on yourself or God, don't give in to Satan and his gimmicks, take all the reports of the experts to the Lord, He has the last say in your case (Habakkuk 2:2). God who sent His blessings through Eli is still sending messages of life, hope, comfort and blessing through His servants, divine revelations and the Word (2 Chronicles 20:20b, Psalm 107:20). Your breakthrough is in your prayers and a word from God is all that is required for your miracle to be birthed.

Some of contents of this chapter are taken from *Provocation, Prayer and Praise* by O. Ola-Ojo and used with the permission of Protokos Publishers.

# EXERCISE TWO

## Evaluate your life from Hannah's story:

**A.**

1. Identify if you have a long standing problem that is known or unknown to your husband.


2. In what ways does your husband show that he loves you?

    a.
    b.
    c.

3. Thank God for giving you a loving and supporting husband.


4. Hannah got her first child through intercession not through strife, fighting/quarrelling, anger, jealousy, malice, etc. What in your character or attitude may cause your husband/family/friends to resent you? Repent of those things you have identified.

5. Examine if you have lost your appetite for food or zeal for life and seek matured Christian counselling immediately. Write down the names of two people you can go to see right away. Contact them now.

   a.

   b.

**B.**

1. List three reasons why you attend or don't attend Church services or fellowship meetings.

   a.

   b.

   c.

2. Despite her problem Hannah continued to go and worship God in the temple in Shiloh every year. Tick those godly things you have stopped doing because of how you feel about your problem.

   ☐ Praying
   ☐ Reading the Word
   ☐ Going to Church
   ☐ Believing in the Word of God
   ☐ Obeying the Word of God
   ☐ Singing/Praising God
   ☐ Spreading the Gospel

- ❑ Giving to the needy
- ❑ Other

3. Examine where you have gone to seek for help and what has been your attitude towards God on the issue.

4. If you have been to any ungodly person/ medium you need to repent of that action now.

**C.**

1. What miracle do you believe God for that will permanently silence your mockers?

2. Hannah's prayer did not need to be lengthy or loud to get God's attention; it was simply focused. For each prayer request you have, write down in one sentence, the specific thing(s) you want God to do for you.

   a.
   b.
   c.
   d.
   e.

3. Present your requests as listed above to Jesus from your heart not necessarily from your lips.

4. Ask the Holy Spirit to comfort and direct you from now on.

**D.**

1. In that which you are trusting God for, what can you do to improve the situation (self improvement)?

   a.
   b.
   c.
   d.
   e.

2. What will you want God to help you achieve?

   a.
   b.
   c.

3. Personally locate two scripture verses, which can help you in each identified area.

a.

b.

c.

d.

e.

4. Write the Scriptures on postcards. Read, memorise and meditate on them. Put the scriptures to test in your life and patiently wait for God's manifestation.

5. Hannah was a promise keeper. Examine if you have made any promise to God that you have not kept. Repent of this now and ask Him to forgive you.

6. Hannah named her son Samuel as a way of acknowledging to the whole world that God was the source of her blessing. In what other ways can you demonstrate that your blessing or miracle is a result of answered prayer?

a.

b.

c.

## Chapter 2 - No One But Jesus

## Prayer For Help

*Dear FATHER, in the name of JESUS CHRIST, I thank YOU that I can come to YOU in times like this. FATHER, in bitterness of soul and in tears, I cry to YOU today in prayers that, O Lord of hosts, if THOU wilt indeed look on the affliction of thine handmaid, and remember me, and not forget thine handmaid, but wilt give unto thine handmaid (please insert your desire here….), with YOUR help I vow to give YOU alone the praise and worship that is due to YOU. (You may make other vows, but be sure you will redeem them when the time comes or better still say nothing now).*

*Thank YOU LORD, for giving me the faith to believe only your report about my situation; for giving me the grace to continue to wait upon YOU; for giving me the patience to tarry for the vision; for giving me the joy and strength for this difficult times; for helping me to do my part and for trusting YOU that YOU will do YOUR part and honour YOUR words in my life; for accepting me and loving me just as I am, in JESUS name I pray with thanksgiving. Amen.*

CHAPTER THREE

# Casting All Upon Him

THERE IS NO HUMAN being without a problem. The problems are only different in types and severity. Why should you continue bearing these problems when you can safely cast all upon the Lord? The more you hide that particular problem of yours, the bigger it will certainly become from experience. So, why won't you share it today with the Saviour, who is anxiously and willingly ready to solve it for you?

Moses was born at a time when the decree forbade male children. Being an unusually beautiful baby, his mother hid him at home. What should have been a natural source of joy and happiness, became a big problem and burden to his parents. His mother out of love, hid him for three months after birth. However Moses was getting bigger and his voice was becoming stronger.

When she could no longer hide him because of the decree, she made a basket from papyrus reed, water-proofed with tar, and put him in that basket along the river edge. She left him there and returned to her home, possibly without any hope of seeing her child again, or conversely, hoping in God for a miraculous preservation of the child's life. God in His infinite plan and love for the Israelites saved Moses' life through one of Pharaoh's daughters. Not only that, he was given to a woman who was paid to nurse him, and this nurse happened to be his real mother. He was also trained as Pharaoh's grandson—a potential heir to the throne.

If you will today believe in the infinite power of God and will openly cast all your cares and burdens upon Him, completely leaving them at the foot of the cross of Calvary, you will experience His divine intervention and solution in your life and circumstance.

Copyright © O. Ola-Ojo 19/06/90. Based on Exodus 2: 1-10

# JOCHEBED

Jochebed was the mother of Moses. She saw that he was a beautiful child and so hid him for three months instead of giving him up to be killed by an ungodly decree. She planned a creative way to give up her son, trusting in God to watch over him.

## HER STORY

*These are the sons of Jacob who went with their father to Egypt, each with his family: Reuben, Simeon, Levi, Judah,*

## Chapter 3 - Casting All Upon Him

*Issachar, Zebulun, Benjamin, Dan, Naphtali, Gadazxzz, and Asher. Joseph was already down in Egypt. In all, Jacob had seventy direct descendants. In time, Joseph and each of his brothers died, ending that generation.*

*But their descendants had many children and grandchildren. In fact, they multiplied so quickly that they soon filled the land. Then a new king came to the throne of Egypt who knew nothing about Joseph or what he had done.*

*He told his people, "These Israelites are becoming a threat to us because there are so many of them. We must find a way to put an end to this. If we don't and if war breaks out, they will join our enemies and fight against us. Then they will escape from the country." So the Egyptians made the Israelites their slaves and put brutal slave drivers over them, hoping to wear them down under heavy burdens. They forced them to build the cities of Pithom and Rameses as supply centers for the king.*

*But the more the Egyptians oppressed them, the more quickly the Israelites multiplied! The Egyptians soon became alarmed and decided to make their slavery more bitter still. They were ruthless with the Israelites, forcing them to make bricks and mortar and to work long hours in the fields. Then Pharaoh, the king of Egypt, gave this order to the Hebrew midwives, Shiphrah and Puah: "When you help the Hebrew women give birth, kill all the boys as soon as they are born. Allow only the baby girls to live."*

*But because the midwives feared God, they refused to obey*

the king and allowed the boys to live, too. Then the king called for the midwives. "Why have you done this?" he demanded. "Why have you allowed the boys to live?" "Sir," they told him, "the Hebrew women are very strong. They have their babies so quickly that we cannot get there in time! They are not slow in giving birth like Egyptian women."

So God blessed the midwives, and the Israelites continued to multiply, growing more and more powerful. And because the midwives feared God, he gave them families of their own. Then Pharaoh gave this order to all his people: "Throw all the newborn Israelite boys into the Nile River. But you may spare the baby girls."

During this time, a man and woman from the tribe of Levi got married. The woman became pregnant and gave birth to a son. She saw what a beautiful baby he was and kept him hidden for three months. But when she could no longer hide him, she got a little basket made of papyrus reeds and waterproofed it with tar and pitch. She put the baby in the basket and laid it among the reeds along the edge of the Nile River.

The baby's sister then stood at a distance, watching to see what would happen to him. Soon after this, one of Pharaoh's daughters came down to bathe in the river, and her servant girls walked along the riverbank. When the princess saw the little basket among the reeds, she told one of her servant girls to get it for her. As the princess opened it, she found the baby boy. His helpless cries touched her heart. "He must be one of the Hebrew *children," she said. Then the baby's sister approached the princess. "Should I go and find one of the Hebrew women to nurse the baby for you?" she asked. "Yes, do!" the princess replied.*

*So the girl rushed home and called the baby's mother. "Take this child home and nurse him for me," the princess told her. "I will pay you for your help." So the baby's mother took her baby home and nursed him. Later, when he was older, the child's mother brought him back to the princess, who adopted him as her son. The princess named him Moses, for she said, "I drew him out of the water." (Exodus 1:1-end; 2:1-10, NLT)*

## UNPLEASANT BIRTH CIRCUMSTANCES

The male seed is very important for the continuity of life and the defence of it. Eliminating the Hebrew boys by Pharaoh's decree would stop Israel from being a threat to Egypt. It was during this frightening period that Amran and Jochebed, a couple from the tribe of Levi—the tribe chosen by God to be His priests—had a baby boy. What should have been an occasion for public celebration turned out for this couple a secret, trying time. It must have been especially difficult for Jochebed who had no say in determining the sex of her child.

Just as there was an ungodly decree against the boys born to the Israelites in the above text, so is it today. The devil has not changed his strategy; he has only re-packaged the method. Male children are often the targets of the enemy in any culture, tribe or society that he wants to eliminate. Over the years in my professional experience, I have observed that many problematic pregnancies are either strategic children or baby boys. For these children, the battle for survival starts from the womb and it takes God and often, good medical care for them to be born alive and healthy. I don't know why and perhaps this is worth researching.

## All Sexes Are Equal

There is no record or evidence that Jochebed complained about the sex of her child. Just as she gladly accepted her baby, so must we, irrespective of sex or any other feature. In God's programme for the world every child has a specific purpose and destiny to fulfil. He knows every child before they are formed in the womb and each one is special to Him (Jeremiah 1:4-5; Psalms 139:13-16).

How sad to see some parents unhappy about the sex of their child! It is an act of ingratitude, wickedness and underestimation of the child. Such parents act as if they are smarter than God and know the end of their child. If you are one of such parents, repent now and ask God for His forgiveness, mercy and grace to love your child from now on. From my little experience of life, it is often the despised child who, with the help of God and his or her personal struggle, ends up sustaining the family at critical times.

## Each Child, A Special Gift

God choose not to reveal to this couple the destiny of their child but his mother saw that he was a "goodly child." Another translation says, "beautiful child" (Exodus 2:2). This was her third child and second son yet she found time to appreciate the baby's unique beauty. Parents please take time to appreciate your children as individuals. Each child is a special gift from God.

To avoid having regrets in future, treat each of your children as a celebrity; God's own ambassador to your home. There should be no comparison with any other person within or outside the family, dead or alive. Genetically only identical twins look alike but then each twin's destiny is often not the same.

In love for her son, Moses' biological mother hid him for three months, nursing him secretly and not giving him up to be thrown into the Nile. The Bible does not say that Moses had a name before the princess gave him one. Circumcision and christening of baby boys usually occur on the eighth day, but this baby was not christened probably to hide his sex from the people around.

Moses' parents were of the tribe of Levi, God's appointed priests, but despite their high calling and anointing, they were not exempted from Pharaoh's ungodly edict. Similarly, children of God today are most times not immune from ungodly decrees in society. Parents need to protect their children's lives from ungodly laws.

## Prayerful Planning

Despite her love and care, Jochebed could no longer hide her son. It was time to let him go so that God could take over. There comes a time mother, when you have to let go of that child and let God step in. This time might come earlier for some than for others but it does surely come for all parents at one point or the other. It may be frightening and worrisome but until you let go and let God, He may not step in.

Jochebed prayerfully planned how to give her child up trusting in God. Instead of throwing him into the Nile as decreed, she made a papyrus basket and plastered it with bitumen and pitch. It was eye catching and comfortable like a little ship. She made sure the basket was waterproof and balanced enough such that the boy's kicking will not overturn it. She put the child in it and placed it among the reeds in a fairly secured part of the Nile River.

Jochebed might have disguised herself to get the basket to the River Nile without attracting attention and returned home to prayerfully wait. Her daughter Miriam stood at

## Chapter 3 - Casting All Upon Him

a distance to see what would happen to the baby in the basket (Exodus 2:3-4). Pharaoh's daughter saw the basket, adopted the baby and decided to appoint a Hebrew woman as the boy's nurse. His sister Miriam went and called their mother for the job. Jochebed was waiting expectantly at home not at the market or the farm when Miriam came to call her for the princess!

This God fearing mother most certainly tutored Miriam on where to be, what to say and what to do—she obviously carried her family along with her in her planning. Training any child will always pay off sooner or later I can assure you of that. Who knows how many prayers this mother said before getting an insight into what to do to save her son? She probably remembered the story of Noah and the ark. Just as there was safety in the ark when the earth was destroyed by water, she believed there would be safety in the basket she made for her son.

Jochebed must have observed how often, when and where the princess usually had her bath in the river. She also must have trusted God to touch the princess' heart on behalf of her son seeing that she could not go openly to her for help. Moses' mother put a lot of time, planning and prayers into getting her son saved despite what was happening to all other male children.

Mum, you too can save your child from ungodly and destructive decrees and acts. If you would only dare to call on God for help and rely on the Holy Spirit for wisdom, favour and mercy, your child can still be saved, healed or delivered. God never leaves His own no wonder the Psalmist said, ...*even though I walk through the darkest valley or in the valley of the shadow of death, I fear no evil for Thou art with me, Your rod and Staff comfort me (Psalms 23:4).*

By God's perfect timing, divine appointment and intervention, Pharaoh's daughter came to bathe in the river Nile, saw the basket, opened it, heard the baby boy cry and took pity on him (Exodus 2:5-6). God hears the cries of children too.

Parents ought to teach their children how to cry to God as early as possible in life (Genesis 21:15 – 17). The same water that killed other boys spared the life of Jochebed's son. The same King that ordered all new born baby boys to be killed adopted Moses to be brought up within the walls of the palace. When the Lord steps into a situation, what was meant to kill and destroy becomes the stepping-stone to victory, protection, provision and fame.

## "Take", "Nurse" And Be Paid

As Pharaoh's daughter said to Jochebed, so says God to parents today, take that child and nurse him/her for me, and I will give you your wages (Exodus 2:9). To "take" in this context means to accept, accommodate, carry, and understand the child just as he or she is without complaint. Not every child will be exceptionally brilliant, athletic or sporty nevertheless look for the God given strong qualities in that child and commend such. Love the child and avoid destructive comparison. To "nurse" in this context means to breast-feed, care for, cherish, encourage, nourish, nurture, promote, support, sustain, and tend the child. To nurse is to feed physically, emotionally, socially and spiritually.

You need to love your children, spend time with them, and be their friend and confidant. Remember that God has given them to you to nurse for Him. The first step to godly parenting is for you to give your life to Jesus and experience His forgiveness, love and mercy. The second step is, to daily depend on Him and His wisdom.

Pharaoh's daughter promised to give Jochebed her wages; even so God is going to reward each mother according to her deeds. He neither sleeps nor slumbers, He watches over every child and is watching how faithful you are as a parent. You may justify your actions but God looks at your motive.

## IMPART YOUR UNIQUE HERITAGE

By the time Moses was given to his biological mother to be nursed, Pharaoh's daughter had adopted him and so in principle he was no longer a Hebrew child. The Bible did not tell us how many years Moses spent with his mother but it certainly was limited. Yet within that time his biological mother/nurse imparted in him among other things, high value for his Hebrew root (see Exodus 2:11-13). Every culture has its unique language, food, traditional costume etc., but it is sad to see some immigrants living in a foreign country refuse to teach their children about their roots, their rich culture and mother tongue.

Ironically, when some of these children grow up, they pay outsiders money to learn various aspects of their own parents' tradition and culture. Being born in another country possibly richer than your home country and having that foreign country's birth certificate does not and will not remove your child from his or her original root. No nation, race or culture is less or more superior to the other.

## Impart The Knowledge Of God

While you teach your children about their cultural root, it is very important not to forget to teach them about their spiritual root as well (Romans 10:13-15, 17). A number of Christian parents are giving their children all that money can buy, sometimes even getting into debt, yet they teach them nothing about God. Many parents are busy making wealth while the media plays the role of nanny and adviser.

In some Christian homes, the only contact the children have with God is in Sunday school. It is interesting to see parents who bear Biblical names but have no idea what those names mean. They in turn give those Biblical names to their children still not knowing the meaning or the Bible personality who bore the name.

Not too long ago, I had a conversation with a mother about her beautiful baby girl. When asked for the name of her daughter, she replied, "Esther." On hearing this, I asked, "You mean like Queen Esther in the Bible?" She was pleasantly surprised and asked me if indeed Esther was a queen in the Bible. I confirmed this and politely told her to visit their family Bible to read it herself. That experience was not the first of its kind that I would have.

## INVEST TIME

As parents, the time we have with our children is limited for soon it will be time for them to go to school, college, University and so on. The greatest investment parents can give to their children is to teach and train them in the way of the Lord particularly before they start school where the world is waiting to bombard them with lots of ungodly information. We ought to make the best use of the time that we have now: *Train up a child in the way he should go: and when he is old, he will not depart from it* (Proverbs 22:6). This is a command from God not a suggestion.

It is a command primarily to parents and secondarily to those who come in contact with and have responsibilities to carry out in the life of children. Children are able to understand the gospel message if we but teach them. They don't lack intelligence they simply lack teachers. Take note of God's admonition and be careful to obey it—*And thou shalt teach them diligently unto thy children, and shalt talk of them when thou sittest in thine house, and when thou walkest by the way, and when thou liest down, and when thou risest up* (Deuteronomy 6:7).

Mother do you need wisdom to nurse your child? *If any of you lack wisdom, let him ask of God, that giveth to all men liberally, and upbraideth not; and it shall be given him. But let him ask in faith, nothing wavering. For he that wavereth is like a wave of the sea driven with the wind and tossed. For let not that man think that he shall receive any thing of the Lord. A double minded man is unstable in all his ways* (James 1:5-8). He, who has chosen you to nurse that child, is well able to equip you for the task if only you will go to Him in prayer (Matthew 7:7-10).

Most of this chapter has been taken from *There is a Reward for Parenting!* by O. Ola-Ojo. Used with permission from *Protokos Publishers*.

Chapter 3 - Casting All Upon Him

# EXERCISE THREE

## Evaluate your life from Jochebed' story:

**A.**

1. List as many ungodly decrees that you know have been set up against children today.

    a.
    b.
    c.
    d.
    e.
    f.
    g.

2. List the ungodly decrees that have been set up to destroy your own child(ren) and those of the household of faith.

    a.
    b.
    c.

3. Identify how you as a mother can combat those ungodly decrees you listed above.

    a.
    b.

c.

   d.

   e.

4. Begin to intercede for the lives of these children. Write down the names of two other mothers you know who can come together with you to pray on these issues right away. Contact them.

   a.

   b.

**B.**

1. Identify all that is not making you to celebrate any of your children e.g. known medical, physical, emotional, spiritual or financial problems.

   a.

   b.

   c.

2. Locate two or three scriptures that will help you to pray about the above.

   a.

   b.

   c.

Memorize the two scriptures and meditate on them.

3. Admit any previous wrong confession, murmuring and complaining regarding that child and ask God to forgive you.

4. If you have inwardly rejected yours or any other person's child because of gender, disability or "unplanned" conception, then confess and repent of it now in Jesus name.

**C.**

1. Begin to appreciate God in each of your children and let each child know how special and unique he or she is.

2. In what way(s) do you have to "let go and let God" in the lives of your children?

    a.
    b.
    c.
    d.
    e.

3. How well have you nursed your children for the Lord? Are you making out time to train them line by line, precept upon precept? Or is it, the television, video, game board, agony, aunt/uncle, Internet or instructor, that is doing the training for you?

4. If God were to give you wages for each child you nurse will you expect a good pay or not? Why or why not?

**D.**

1. In what ways have you been comparing your children with their siblings or other people's children?

2. Identify and pray about the strongest points in each of your children. (List and pray for each child's strengths separately.)

   a.
   b.
   c.
   d.

3. Identify and pray about the weaknesses in each of your children. (List and pray for each child's weak areas separately.)

   a.

   b.

   c.

4. In what ways have you been underestimating any of your children?

   a.

   b.

   c.

**E.**

1. In which areas have you been struggling with bringing up your child(ren) in the Lord?

   a.

   b.

   c.

2. Ask God for His cleansing and empowerment so you can be all that He wants you to be in life.

## Prayer For Help

*Dear FATHER, in the name of JESUS CHRIST, I thank YOU for the privilege of examining my life in the light of the life of Jochebed, the mother of Moses. Thank YOU LORD for the conception of our child(ren) (mention name(s)) and his/her/their arrival at YOUR own timing. Help me LORD to be able to appreciate your beauty in him/her/them. I bring before YOU these ungodly decree(s) that want to terminate the life/lives of our child(ren) and I ask in JESUS name for YOUR counsel on how to overcome them.*

*Please help me LORD to invest good quality time in our children's upbringing, teaching them, among other things, the fear of the LORD. I need YOUR wisdom in this matter and YOUR own divine instruction.*

*Please LORD, help me to be a good mother and trusted friend to our children, in JESUS name I have prayed, and with thanksgiving. Amen.*

CHAPTER FOUR
# In The Twinkling Of An Eye

THE ALMIGHTY GOD IS so big, so strong and powerful. Such is the greatness, faithfulness and grace of God. Such that he brings to pass things that are not "just in the twinkling of an eye," you may say, my brother. The whole world and all it contains as we know today was spoken into existence we read from the Bible—light and darkness, sun and moon, land and sea, all came to be "just in the twinkling of an eye."

Rebecca the shepherdess, on her normal daily duty, gave water to a stranger and watered his camels. "In the twinkling of an eye," she became engaged and thereafter got married to Isaac, the multi-millionaire. Joseph, the slave imprisoned by Potiphar unjustly must have lost all hope of freedom and leadership. Interpreting dreams to troubled Pharaoh years later made him the first Prime Minister, just "in the twinkling of an eye."

Moses, who was doomed to die at birth in Egypt, and laid in a basket with love among the river reeds, became Pharaoh's grandson with all the fringe benefits "just in the twinkling of an eye," as soon as the Princess found him. The woman with the issue of blood, the Bible recalls, had suffered for twelve years spending all she had. What a joy of healing and relief she must have experienced, "Just in the twinkling of an eye," after touching the hem of Jesus' garment. The bent woman at the temple on a Sabbath say received total healing "just in the twinkling of an eye," as Jesus commanded forgiveness and healing to her.

How dramatic and unbelievable the miracle must have appeared. That problem that has bugged you for so long, my brother, my sister; that promise that has been delayed and almost forgotten, be prepared to be relieved "just in the twinkling of an eye." God's miracles mostly come "just in the twinkling of an eye." The second coming of our Lord Jesus Christ, the Bible says, will be like His first departure, like a thief in the night, "just in the twinkling of an eye," we all shall be transformed. Better be prepared, for no one knows where and when.

Copyright © O. Ola-Ojo 26/03/90

# REBECCA

Rebecca initially suffered from primary infertility. Her husband interceded on her behalf and God gave her twins but each parent favoured one child over the other and this caused trouble between the twins.

CHAPTER 4 - IN THE TWINKLING OF AN EYE

# HER STORY

*This is the history of the family of Isaac, the son of Abraham. When Isaac was forty years old, he married Rebekah, the daughter of Bethuel the Aramean from Paddan-aram and the sister of Laban. Isaac pleaded with the Lord to give Rebekah a child because she was childless. So the Lord answered Isaac's prayer, and his wife became pregnant with twins.*

*But the two children struggled with each other in her womb. So she went to ask the Lord about it. "Why is this happening to me?" she asked. And the Lord told her, "The sons in your womb will become two rival nations. One nation will be stronger than the other; the descendants of your older son will serve the descendants of your younger son."*

*And when the time came, the twins were born. The first was very red at birth. He was covered with so much hair that one would think he was wearing a piece of clothing. So they called him Esau. Then the other twin was born with his hand grasping Esau's heel. So they called him Jacob. Isaac was sixty years old when the twins were born. As the boys grew up, Esau became a skilful hunter, a man of the open fields, while Jacob was the kind of person who liked to stay at home. Isaac loved Esau in particular because of the wild game he brought home, but Rebekah favored Jacob.*

*One day when Jacob was cooking some stew, Esau arrived home exhausted and hungry from a hunt. Esau said to Jacob,*

*"I'm starved! Give me some of that red stew you've made." (This was how Esau got his other name, Edom—"Red.") Jacob replied, "All right, but trade me your birthright for it." "Look, I'm dying of starvation!" said Esau. "What good is my birthright to me now?"*

*So Jacob insisted, "Well then, swear to me right now that it is mine." So Esau swore an oath, thereby selling all his rights as the firstborn to his younger brother. Then Jacob gave Esau some bread and lentil stew. Esau ate and drank and went on about his business, indifferent to the fact that he had given up his birthright. (Genesis 25:19-34)*

*When Isaac was old and almost blind, he called for Esau, his older son, and said, "My son?" "Yes, Father?" Esau replied. "I am an old man now," Isaac said, "and I expect every day to be my last. Take your bow and a quiver full of arrows out into the open country, and hunt some wild game for me. Prepare it just the way I like it so it's savoury and good, and bring it here for me to eat. Then I will pronounce the blessing that belongs to you, my firstborn son, before I die."*

*But Rebekah overheard the conversation. So when Esau left to hunt for the wild game, she said to her son Jacob, "I overheard your father asking Esau to prepare him a delicious meal of wild game. He wants to bless Esau in the Lord's presence before he dies. Now, my son, do exactly as I tell you. Go out to the flocks and bring me two fine young goats. I'll prepare your father's favorite dish from them. Take the food to your father; then he can*

## Chapter 4 - In The Twinkling Of An Eye

*eat it and bless you instead of Esau before he dies." "But Mother!" Jacob replied. "He won't be fooled that easily. Think how hairy Esau is and how smooth my skin is! What if my father touches me? He'll see that I'm trying to trick him, and then he'll curse me instead of blessing me." "Let the curse fall on me, dear son," said Rebekah. "Just do what I tell you. Go out and get the goats."*

*So Jacob followed his mother's instructions, bringing her the two goats. She took them and cooked a delicious meat dish, just the way Isaac liked it. Then she took Esau's best clothes, which were there in the house, and dressed Jacob with them. She made him a pair of gloves from the hairy skin of the young goats, and she fastened a strip of the goat's skin around his neck. Then she gave him the meat dish, with its rich aroma, and some freshly baked bread.*

*Jacob carried the platter of food to his father and said, "My father?" "Yes, my son," he answered. "Who is it-Esau or Jacob?" Jacob replied, "It's Esau, your older son. I've done as you told me. Here is the wild game, cooked the way you like it. Sit up and eat it so you can give me your blessing." Isaac asked, "How were you able to find it so quickly, my son?" "Because the Lord your God put it in my path!" Jacob replied.*

*Then Isaac said to Jacob, "Come over here. I want to touch you to make sure you really are Esau." So Jacob went over to his father, and Isaac touched him. "The voice is Jacob's, but the hands are Esau's," Isaac said to himself. But he did not recognize Jacob because Jacob's hands felt hairy just like Esau's. So Isaac* pronounced his blessing on Jacob. "Are you really my son Esau?" he asked. "Yes, of course," Jacob replied. Then Isaac said, "Now, my son, bring me the meat. I will eat it, and then I will give you my blessing."

So Jacob took the food over to his father, and Isaac ate it. He also drank the wine that Jacob served him. Then Isaac said, "Come here and kiss me, my son." So Jacob went over and kissed him. And when Isaac caught the smell of his clothes, he was finally convinced, and he blessed his son. He said, "The smell of my son is the good smell of the open fields that the Lord has blessed.

May God always give you plenty of dew for healthy crops and good harvests of grain and wine. May many nations become your servants. May you be the master of your brothers. May all your mother's sons bow low before you. All who curse you are cursed, and all who bless you are blessed." As soon as Isaac had blessed Jacob, and almost before Jacob had left his father, Esau returned from his hunting trip.

Esau prepared his father's favorite meat dish and brought it to him. Then he said, "I'm back, Father, and I have the wild game. Sit up and eat it so you can give me your blessing." But Isaac asked him, "Who are you?" "Why, it's me, of course!" he replied. "It's Esau, your older son." Isaac began to tremble uncontrollably and said, "Then who was it that just served me wild game? I have already eaten it, and I blessed him with an irrevocable blessing before you came."

## Chapter 4 - In The Twinkling Of An Eye

*When Esau understood, he let out a loud and bitter cry. "O my father, bless me, too!" he begged. But Isaac said, "Your brother was here, and he tricked me. He has carried away your blessing." Esau said bitterly, "No wonder his name is Jacob, for he has deceived me twice, first taking my birthright and now stealing my blessing. Oh, haven't you saved even one blessing for me?" Isaac said to Esau, "I have made Jacob your master and have declared that all his brothers will be his servants. I have guaranteed him an abundance of grain and wine-what is there left to give?" Esau pleaded, "Not one blessing left for me? O my father, bless me, too!" Then Esau broke down and wept.*

*His father, Isaac, said to him, "You will live off the land and what it yields, and you will live by your sword. You will serve your brother for a time, but then you will shake loose from him and be free." Esau hated Jacob because he had stolen his blessing, and he said to himself, "My father will soon be dead and gone. Then I will kill Jacob."*

*But someone got wind of what Esau was planning and reported it to Rebekah. She sent for Jacob and told him, "Esau is threatening to kill you. This is what you should do. Flee to your uncle Laban in Haran. Stay there with him until your brother's fury is spent. When he forgets what you have done, I will send for you. Why should I lose both of you in one day?" Then Rebekah said to Isaac, "I'm sick and tired of these local Hittite women. I'd rather die than see Jacob marry one of them." (Genesis 27:1-46, NLT)*

## Ante Natal Prayer

Rebecca had some rough times during her pregnancy and decided to seek the face of the Lord concerning this.

In response to her prayer, God told her that she was carrying twin sons and also revealed the destiny of each of them (That was a long time before the era of ultrasound scans). We serve a God who is willing to share His plans and thoughts with us (Genesis 18:17-19). Take time to seek the face of the Lord in prayers concerning your pregnancy and once He has spoken continue to pray for the baby(ies) in your womb.

## Beware Of Favouritism

For whatever reasons, Rebecca and Isaac decided to show favouritism. She chose Jacob as her favourite whilst Isaac chose Esau (Genesis 25:24-28).

Unfortunately this entrenched disunity, envy, jealousy, and unnecessary rivalry and even untimely death amongst her children (Genesis 37:3, 19-20). Can you truly say as a mother of more than one child that you have not shown favouritism to any one of your children?

I know a family with more than one child where both parents in wisdom have refused to have an overall best child, rather they might say in cleaning the house child number one is the best but in giving a helping hand in the kitchen, child number three is best. That way none of the children feels left out and there is no ugly jealousy amongst them.

## Leave God To Take Charge

Isaac in preparation for his death at a ripe old age decided to pronounce blessings on Esau his firstborn as must have been customary in those days. (Genesis 27:1-46; 28:5)

Rebecca heard the discussion between Isaac and Esau and whilst Esau went out to carry out his father's instruction before receiving his blessing, she called Jacob and connived with him to deny Esau of his biological right.

Could she have done this because she remembered God's choice of Jacob over Esau from when they were in the womb? Perhaps she had never shared this revelation with Isaac or Isaac deliberately ignored the revelation forcing Rebecca to play pranks to get God's will done for Jacob at all cost. Rebecca was not present in the room with Isaac when he was talking to Esau about blessing him, so it could be that there was a communication gap between both parents.

Whatever the case, Rebecca strongly felt that she needed to help God by organising that Jacob received the blessing of the first born instead of Esau. She even went as far as agreeing to be cursed instead of Jacob should Isaac find out their deception! Mothers, please be assured God can fulfil His promises concerning your child without your ungodly help. Rebecca took advantage of her husband's poor eyesight, and helped in obtaining blessings for her favourite son by deceit. Exploiting the fact that she knew what appealed to her husband's taste buds, she cheated by cooking him his favourite meal the way she knew he would like it.

Against Esau's knowledge, she took his best clothes and gave them to Jacob to wear thereby betraying Esau's trust in her. In the same way, some mothers today have betrayed their children's trust in them by unnecessarily opening them up to wicked people. Some have, without the child's knowledge, given out his or her things to those who will use such articles against them.

## Are You A Peace Maker Or Breaker?

When Rebecca realised how furious Esau was and the possibility of Jacob being hurt or killed by him, she suggested to her husband that Jacob be sent away to her brother Laban to get a wife. In actual fact she was secretly hoping that the distance and time would appease Esau's anger. In the end, she did not live to see Jacob return home. There is no account in the Bible of Rebecca explaining or apologising to Esau for the trauma she caused him. Rebecca here was not a peacemaker but a peace breaker.

## Chapter 4 - In The Twinkling Of An Eye

Many mothers have destroyed their homes and the lives of their children by favouritism. Other mothers use divide and rule tactics among their children. Both are sinful acts that need to be confessed and dealt with.

To Esau, Rebecca was probably not the best of mothers but to Jacob she was the best mother he could have had. She helped him to get the first born inheritance that traditionally should have gone to Esau, wisely sent him with Isaac's approval to his Uncle Laban where he not only met but married wives, had eleven boys and a girl, acquired so much herds, servants and wealth. Rebecca indirectly launched Jacob into his destiny at the cost of her life.

# EXERCISE FOUR

**Evaluate your life from Rebecca's story:**

**A.**

1. Is it possible to love your children equally? Why or why not?



2. List the various possible ways a mother can show favouritism amongst her children.

   a.
   b.
   c.
   d.
   e.

3. Examine your relationship with your children and see which of them you have favoured in any of the ways mentioned above.

4. Do you tend to compare your children?

5. If yes, in what areas/aspects of their lives do you do so most?

6. What effect has this had on your children? (You may want to talk with them about this individually).

7. Identify what practical steps you can take to repair the damage(s) done by your acts of favouritism.

**B.**

1. In what ways have you plotted with any of your children against the other?

2. Repent and ask for God's forgiveness and the forgiveness of your children now.

3. Ask God for wisdom on how to show equal love to your children.

**C.**

Who among your children have you connived with to defraud any other child of their inheritance and why?

1. List the ways you have knowingly or unknowingly pronounced curses on yourself, family or children and why.

    a.

    b.

    c.

2. Confess your sins to God and choose to speak life, health and goodness into your family from now on.

**D.**

1. Have you played divide and rule amongst your children? If so, state when and why?

    | **When:** | **Why:** |
    |---|---|
    | a. | |
    | b. | |
    | c. | |

2. In what ways have you betrayed the trust of your children?

3. Repent and ask for the children's forgiveness and God's forgiveness.

## Prayer For Help

**Fruitfulness/Pregnancy:**

*Dear FATHER, in the name of JESUS CHRIST, I thank YOU for the privilege of examining my life in the light of the life of Rebecca. FATHER, I bring before YOU the challenge of inability to conceive/difficulty in this pregnancy. I am grateful to YOU that YOU know me and You are abundantly able to save, deliver and bless me in this situation. YOUR word says I will not be barren nor miscarry and that the blessings of the LORD makes rich and adds no sorrow to it. LORD I thank YOU for the testimony of my successful conception and delivery in Jesus name.*

**Raising Your Children:**

*FATHER, I confess that I have shown favouritism amongst*

*our children. On other occasions, I have played divide and rule amongst our children and have hurt (name them) by my actions. Please LORD, forgive me and help me to act positively from now on. Thank YOU FATHER for answered prayers in JESUS name I pray and with thanksgiving. (AMEN)*

CHAPTER FIVE

# God's Gift You Can Never Buy

FRIEND, HAVE YOU EVER thought about something? I mean about God's numerous gifts to mankind? Isn't God wonderful and generous to you and me? All His gifts to mankind, He gave free of charge. Beginning with life itself, it is free to mankind. Money can buy medicine and care, but not life or health. The air we breathe in is abundance and free everywhere. Can you imagine if we have to pay for that in a day?

Nothing quenches thirst as much as ordinary water, yet God has made it available to man in abundance. The radiant sun breaks the dawn and shines bright. All living things depend on it for their growth and vitality.

That pretty baby is a wonderful gift from God. Medicine can help produce test tube babies, yet the sperm and the egg used are really God's. Indeed, you and I can never buy God's gift. Imagine Jesus having to pay the price for our sins on the cross. He was hanged for you and I, shedding His innocent and sinless blood, for no one else qualified for the required atonement. What on earth is equivalent to His shed blood? What can we pay for such an eternal sacrifice? Who among the prophets could stand in the gap to appease God's wrath and justice against the sin of man?

Tell me which power is equal to that of the Holy Spirit? Who is as humble, gentle and powerful as Him? Yet at Pentecost, He was poured on the disciples. And today, He is still empowering Christians.

Simon the sorcerer thought he could buy salvation, and possibly a bit of manifestations of the Holy Ghost, so he asked the apostles for it, offering them money. How foolish for him to have thought such gift can be bought. In the same vein, we probably tried to buy some of God's gifts by the very way we think and live our lives, dear friend. Why not pause and think when next you are tempted. There is no controversy, God's gift you can never buy.

There are not enough riches in the world, says the Bible, to redeem just a single soul from hell fire. There are not enough blankets or scientific discoveries to cover the sun or moon and prevent them from shining. There are not enough works that any man can do to merit salvation, God's free gift to mankind. There is not enough holiness or justification to qualify one automatically for the manifestation of the Holy Ghost.

Whatever you have in life is a gift to you from God.

CHAPTER 5 - GOD'S GIFT YOU CAN NEVER BUY

None of us can pay for any of them, now or later, in cash or kind. With a heart daily full of gratitude, friend, remember God's gift, no matter how small or big, can never be bought with money, fame or affluence.

Copyright © O. Ola Ojo 1992

# THE SHUNAMMITE WOMAN

The woman of Shunem was barren but this did not stop her from being sensitive to other people's needs. She and her husband gave a prophet furnished accommodation and God unexpectedly blessed them with a child.

## HER STORY

*One day Elisha went to the town of Shunem. A wealthy woman lived there, and she invited him to eat some food. From then on, whenever he passed that way, he would stop there to eat. She said to her husband, "I am sure this man who stops in from time to time is a holy man of God. Let's make a little room for him on the roof and furnish it with a bed, a table, a chair, and a lamp. Then he will have a place to stay whenever he comes by."*

*One day Elisha returned to Shunem, and he went up to his room to rest. He said to his servant Gehazi, "Tell the woman I want to speak to her." When she arrived, Elisha said to Gehazi, "Tell her that we appreciate the kind concern she has shown us. Now ask her what we can do for her. Does she want me to put in a good word for her to the king or to the commander of the army?"* "No," she replied, "*my family takes good care of me.*"

Later Elisha asked Gehazi, "What do you think we can do for her?" He suggested, "She doesn't have a son, and her husband is an old man." "Call her back again," Elisha told him. When the woman returned, Elisha said to her as she stood in the doorway, "Next year at about this time you will be holding a son in your arms!" "No, my lord!" she protested. "Please don't lie to me like that, O man of God." But sure enough, the woman soon became pregnant. And at that time the following year she had a son, just as Elisha had said.

One day when her child was older, he went out to visit his father, who was working with the harvesters. Suddenly he complained, "My head hurts! My head hurts!" His father said to one of the servants, "Carry him home to his mother." So the servant took him home, and his mother held him on her lap. But around noontime he died.

She carried him up to the bed of the man of God, then shut the door and left him there. She sent a message to her husband: "Send one of the servants and a donkey so that I can hurry to the man of God and come right back." "Why today?" he asked. "It is neither a new moon festival nor a Sabbath." But she said, "It's all right." So she saddled the donkey and said to the servant, "Hurry! Don't slow down on my account unless I tell you to."

As she approached the man of God at Mount Carmel, Elisha saw her in the distance. He said to Gehazi, "Look, the woman

## Chapter 5 - God's Gift You Can Never Buy

*from Shunem is coming. Run out to meet her and ask her, 'Is everything all right with you, with your husband, and with your child?'" "Yes," the woman told Gehazi, "everything is fine."*

*But when she came to the man of God at the mountain, she fell to the ground before him and caught hold of his feet. Gehazi began to push her away, but the man of God said, "Leave her alone. Something is troubling her deeply, and the Lord has not told me what it is." Then she said, "It was you, my lord, who said I would have a son. And didn't I tell you not to raise my hopes?"*

*Then Elisha said to Gehazi, "Get ready to travel; take my staff and go! Don't talk to anyone along the way. Go quickly and lay the staff on the child's face." But the boy's mother said, "As surely as the Lord lives and you yourself live, I won't go home unless you go with me." So Elisha returned with her.*

*Gehazi hurried on ahead and laid the staff on the child's face, but nothing happened. There was no sign of life. He returned to meet Elisha and told him, "The child is still dead." When Elisha arrived, the child was indeed dead, lying there on the prophet's bed. He went in alone and shut the door behind him and prayed to the Lord. Then he lay down on the child's body, placing his mouth on the child's mouth, his eyes on the child's eyes, and his hands on the child's hands. And the child's body began to grow warm again!*

*Elisha got up and walked back and forth in the room a few times. Then he stretched himself out again on the child. This time the boy sneezed seven times and opened his eyes! Then Elisha summoned Gehazi. "Call the child's mother!" he said. And when she came in, Elisha said, "Here, take your son!" She fell at his feet, overwhelmed with gratitude. Then she picked up her son and carried him downstairs. (2 Kings 4:8-37, NLT)*

## Givers Never Lack

The Bible does not say for how long the woman and her husband had been barren or what attempts they had made to bare a child. One can only infer that being a prominent and well to do couple, they must have tried all available means with no result before resigning themselves to living without a child. This however did not affect the woman's ability to recognise other people's needs and her readiness to meet such needs.

This wealthy but unnamed Shunammite woman invited and persuaded Elisha to have a meal at their house without knowing who he was. She was observant and spoke to her husband about Elisha. With his consent, she provided a comfortable, fully furnished guest room for the prophet and his attendants for their use whenever they were in town.

She generously fed and looked after her guests with no ulterior motive. The woman had totally accepted her barrenness that she did not see it as a need to present to the prophet when she was asked for her desire. Perhaps she had even experienced many failed promises regarding this in the past. When Prophet Elisha told her she would have a child, she quickly replied, "No, my Lord, O man of God, do not lie to your maidservant" (v. 16).

True to the prophet's promise, she had a son the following year (v. 17).

## NOT A TRADE BY BATTER

The Shunammite woman gave without knowing who she was entertaining and when she found out who it was, it did not make her expect or ask for 'special prayers.' What an attitude! She was a woman of dignity, character and great contentment. She did not cash in on her investment in the prophet. She stood at the door not taking advantage of the invitation to come in. Neither did she make advances to the prophet especially with an old husband like hers (v. 15).

A number of women today have been deceived or abused by false prophets and charlatans. Others, confronted with challenging issues, get involved with great men of God who subsequently stumble and fall thereby short-circuiting God's anointing upon their lives and ministry.

God's ways are not our ways. There are stories of couples who after trying all possible means to have children to no avail resign themselves to carry on childless only to conceive later without any human interference. You might have given up on yourself but God has not. He is still in the business of divine intervention.

Keep doing the good that you know to do; God will surely reward you for it. He always remembers our labour of love. Read about Abraham entertaining the strangers in Genesis 18:4-16; Joseph interpreting the dreams in Genesis 40:1-23 and Genesis 41:1-14. You may also read Ecclesiastes 11:1, 5, and 6. Indeed it is not over until God says it is over.

## EMERGENCY! WHAT DO YOU DO?

The miracle baby of the Shunammite woman grew up normally. One day, he went out with his father to the farm and whilst there he suddenly took ill and later on died on his mother's laps. But his mother did not panic nor have a mourning party. She took permission from her husband to go the same day to Elisha, without giving the details of why.

Perhaps there was no time to explain or she did not want to make any negative pronouncement about the state of her son. Maybe she also did not want her husband to delay or stop her or dampen and puncture her faith.

She knew she would find the man of God on Mount Carmel and told the servant not to slow down as he drove her up the hill to see Elisha. She sacrificed her comfort to obtain help for her son as quickly as possible. Every caring mother has on many occasions sacrificed her comfort and pleasure for the sake of her child's immediate and future well-being.

Mum, it is good in emergencies to have someone you can confide in—a man or woman of God whose faith you can tap into and who you can be sure will take a strong spiritual position with you in prayers. Those who have cared to pray and sought for help from the right quarters, have received their dead back alive. What is it that wants to terminate God's destiny for your child? To be conceived by divine revelation and pronouncement does not automatically immune a child from the wicked acts of Satan.

There are times when the problem you face will require the personal involvement of anointed men or women of God. Please do not hesitate to share the problem with those who will lift your weary hands in prayers.

## Positive Declarations

As the Shunammite woman approached the man of God, he sent his servant to ask if all was well to which she replied, "Everything is fine," or in another Bible translation, "It is well". She was not telling lies; she was only declaring her faith by saying how she expected the situation to end. She did not discuss her problem with Gehazi, who Elisha had sent to meet her. She waited to get to the man of God, and caught him by his feet as an act of humility.

Every mother ought to be careful with her confessions especially during times of crisis. What you call forth will come forth. The devil sometimes sets people up to confess negatively about their situation especially when they are stressed. In emergencies you can only use what you have stored. Storing God's word abundantly in your heart gives you something to readily cash in on in time of trouble.

Though Elisha was a man of God and a prophet, the Lord did not forewarn him about the Shunammite woman's predicament. It was when she asked, "Did I desire a son of my lord? Did I not say, Do not deceive me?" that he understood what her problem was. Indeed the secret things belong to God and the things that He chooses to reveal are for us and our children so that we might learn to obey the Lord and the words of His law (Deuteronomy 29:29, paraphrased).

## THE POWER OF PERSISTENCE

Elisha instructed his servant to go and lay his staff upon the face of the child but the Shunammite woman refused to return home without the prophet and she persisted in her request (v. 29,30). She had sown into the life and ministry of the man of God and now she was about to reap from her seed. It is time for you to seek the face of the Lord for wisdom and direction to deal with any dead areas in the life of your children. It is time to seek for counselling and prayers from the right sources on behalf of your children.

Do not be put off by any protocol that might want to prevent you from speaking to the servant of God; persistence pays. Whatever wants to terminate or destroy the testimonies or destiny of your children qualifies for urgent attention. It must not be tolerated.

Elisha raised the dead boy to life and there was no record of the sickness afflicting him again or of him becoming brain dead despite the fact that he had not been alive for quite some time.

The Shunammite woman got her son back alive did not forget to appreciate the man of God (vv. 36-37). Be careful my sister about what you sow into the lives of others for in due season you will reap its fruit. God always remembers whatever you give to Him and His people; He will show up for you in the time of trouble just as He did for the Shunammite woman.

# EXERCISE FIVE

**Evaluate your life from the Shunammite woman's story.**

**A.**

1. How open are you to the needs of those around you?



2. How hospitable are you to visitors and strangers?



3. When people stop by your home unannounced are they sure of getting food to eat?

    ☐ Regularly
    ☐ Sometimes
    ☐ Always
    ☐ Rarely
    ☐ Never

4. Will visitors who stop by your home unannounced have a room to stay?

    ☐ Regularly
    ☐ Sometimes
    ☐ Always

- ❏ Rarely
- ❏ Never

5. Do you take time to involve your husband in your hospitality to visitors and strangers?

- ❏ Daily
- ❏ Regularly
- ❏ Sometimes
- ❏ Rarely
- ❏ Never

**B.**

1. List the unmet needs of your life?

    a.

    b.

    c.

2. In spite of those needs, what positive attributes do you have and how well are you using them?

    a.

    b.

    c.

    d.

    e.

**C.**

1. Identify the dead areas that need to be revived in the life of each of your child(ren) (Write a separate list for each child).

    a.

    b.

    c.

    d.

2. Ask God to give you wisdom and direction to effect a positive change in each of the mentioned areas in the lives of your children.

**D.**

1. What is it that wants to terminate God's destiny for your child or children?

    ❏ Poor health

    ❏ Lack of finances

    ❏ Loneliness

    ❏ Waywardness

    ❏ Stubbornness

    ❏ Laziness

    ❏ Backbiting

## Chapter 5 - God's Gift You Can Never Buy

- ☐ Fear
- ☐ Other

2. Take the issues to God in prayer.

**E.**

1. Identify your limitations as a mother.

   a.
   b.
   c.
   d.
   e.

2. Where can you get appropriate counsel? Begin to seek for help from the right quarters

3. What have you sacrificed e.g. comfort, joy, etc. in order for your child to be better off than yourself?

   a.
   b.
   c.
   d.
   e.

4. What have you offered/sown/given to the people of God and His work that God can remember you by and cause Him to show up for you in the days of your challenge?

   a.

   b.

   c.

## Prayer For Help

*Dear FATHER in heaven, thank YOU that in spite of my challenges, I do have the following which YOU can use (list them) e.g. talent, time, resources, etc., and I pray that YOU will find something however small to use in me.*

*Thank YOU LORD for the gift of our child(ren). I bring before YOU all that is making our child(ren) to be dead or like dead to YOU especially the following areas e.g. education, health, etc. Thank YOU LORD for the presence and ministry of the HOLY SPIRIT. I ask for YOUR help and deliverance.*

*Remember LORD and bless the labour of my love to YOUR Work and Ministers of the Gospel. Let it be a memorial offering to YOU that will attract YOUR blessings and favour in JESUS name I pray and with thanksgiving. Amen.*

CHAPTER SIX
# God's Provision—My Part

GOD HAS ENOUGH PROVISION for all the people in the world that will dare to call upon HIM for help with their needs? In HIS storehouse, there is abundance for dispatch, but each one with a need has a part to play in receiving. In the Garden of Eden, there was an abundance of food fruits, vegetables, fishes, and all types of animal meat, but Adam and Eve had to choose what they wanted to eat. They also had to go and get it for themselves, whenever they are hungry.

God provided manna and quails for the Israelites without failing on a daily basis for forty years on their way to the land of Canaan. However, they had to *collect their meals everyday*, except on the Sabbath. The manna flakes in the morning and quails in the evening.

The widow with her two sons was in great financial distress, but unknown to her, the jar of oil was God's provision for them. So, at the word of the prophet, she went to borrow as many pots and barrels as were available from her neighbours, and behind closed doors, she poured the jar of oil into the vessels until there was none left to fill (see 2 Kings 4:1-7).

The widow of Zarepath and her son were preparing for their very last meal. The famine was very severe in the land with no hope for the next day, but Elijah the prophet demanded that he be served first. Yet, that was the beginning of a feeding programme for both her family and the prophet (see 1 Kings 17:12-16).

Peter and Jesus were unable to pay their taxes when asked. Then Peter was instructed by Jesus to go and fish in the sea and the first fish caught would have money in its mouth enough to pay the taxes of both Jesus and Peter as required.

God has promised to meet that need my brother, my sister. His part for providing for your needs, He would fulfil. My part and your part in receiving would require total obedience to God's instructions as He would graciously reveal. My part and your part, my brother, my sister, in meeting that need require us to identify and accept that we indeed have a need. A need that only God can meet and He is willing to meet as long as we trust in His abundant provision and are obedient to His leading.

Copyright © O. Ola-Ojo 24-25/9/01

# UNNAMED PROPHET'S WIDOW

A poor widow is about to loose her two sons to her

husband's debt collectors. God gives a miracle to pay up the debt and have enough left over to live on with her children.

## Her Story

*One day the widow of one of Elisha's fellow prophets came to Elisha and cried out to him, "My husband who served you is dead, and you know how he feared the Lord. But now a creditor has come, threatening to take my two sons as slaves." "What can I do to help you?" Elisha asked. "Tell me, what do you have in the house?" "Nothing at all, except a flask of olive oil," she replied.*

*And Elisha said, "Borrow as many empty jars as you can from your friends and neighbors. Then go into your house with your sons and shut the door behind you. Pour olive oil from your flask into the jars, setting the jars aside as they are filled. "So she did as she was told. Her sons brought many jars to her, and she filled one after another. Soon every container was full to the brim! "Bring me another jar," she said to one of her sons. "There aren't any more!" he told her. And then the olive oil stopped flowing.*

*When she told the man of God what had happened, he said to her, "Now sell the olive oil and pay your debts, and there will be enough money left over to support you and your sons." (2 Kings 4:1-7, NLT)*

## Why Me Lord?

Why do bad things happen to good people? That is a

question that has been asked over and over again. The Bible introduces this widow as the wife of a prophet who, when he was alive, feared God. Children of God are not immune from physical or social problems.

Jesus said, in this world you will have tribulations and problems but take courage for He has overcome the world (John 16:33). We may not know why, but we do know that nothing happens to any child of God without His knowledge; He is in control of every situation and is glorified through it all.

Since the widow was unable to pay her debts, the creditors decided to take her two sons as slaves instead. Those children were all that she had left. Satan's gimmicks have not changed; he still attacks the homes of God-fearing people and children are usually his first targets. The devil enslaves children through war and occult oppressions such as the Swiss cult and Generation-X (18-25 year olds). The Jason Smith assault and murder (BBC, Tuesday 4/10/94) is another example of the devil at work.

The widow's condition was very desperate. She must have tried to sort herself out and even consulted the financial experts of the day without any positive result. Today's mother in such a situation would have so many options to choose from—the doctor, financial/legal/social adviser, astrologer, palm reader, fortune-teller, or she may decide to play national lottery, pool, etc.?

No matter who you are, there will come a point in

your life when what you face is greater than your ability to handle. That is when you need to move beyond yourself into the loving arms of Jesus. This widow sought for help from the right place and the right person. She cried out loud and clear.

From the world's perspective there are many places you can go to find help and comfort but there is only one place you will find a hand to wipe your tears, and a heart to listen to your every longing. True peace and help come from the Lord God (Psalm 121:1-2). Nothing is so great that God is not greater than. Stop hiding your problems, for problems concealed can kill but problems exposed early and to the right people can be solved.

Come to God as you are and cry out to Him. Jesus said, *"Come unto me, all ye that labour and are heavy laden, and I will give you rest" (Matthew 11:28).* You have the opportunity to call on Him corporately in such places like the Church, prayer meetings and weekly home groups. Please be part of these groups that seek to wait and call on the Lord together. Jesus is the one who is faithful and who is true.

## What You Have Is All You Need

Prophet Elisha in verse 2 asked the widow, *"...what do you have...?"* This widow recognised what she had though little and replied, *"Thine handmaid hath not any thing in the house save a pot of oil.*" In other words, she had nothing except a jar of oil. Whatever your challenge or problem is, sister, if you will search your home and your life well, you will discover that God has left you with at least one "except".

It could be your musical talent, hospitality, painting, drawing, time to pray, good sense of humour, sewing or baking ability, hair dressing or computer skills, cooking, interior decoration, flower arrangements, reading, writing, teaching, book keeping, taking care of the sick or feeble, management, organising events, etc. Stop underestimating your own "except" and avoid comparing your own "except" with that of others. Learn to give your "except" to God.

Unknown to the widow she had an anointing for business which came to lime light through the instruction of the prophet. I believe every woman is anointed for business, even as a housewife or homemaker, as some will prefer to call it. I salute mothers who have taken career breaks to look after their little children, especially in the first five years of the child's life. I am not talking about mothers who sit idle watching soaps and movies and engage in neighbourhood gossip, but mothers who stay at home to actually look after their children and bring them up in the fear of the Lord.

However, the fact that you are a homemaker should not deter you from doing profitable business from home.

What you need is in your home, prepared, and the anointing of God is upon your life already. Ask Him to help you to recognize what you have, and how He wants you to do that business from home. Go for it my sisters, but remember, do not engage in any home business at the expense of your family or your own well-being.

## Seek And Obey Divine Instructions

Prophet Elisha gave the widow instructions on what to do with the pot of oil (v. 3). Mum, there will always be an instruction for you to follow, a command to obey, if you are to overcome your problem. God's ways and thoughts are not like ours (Isaiah 55:9).

This widow was instructed to go and borrow large vessels from all her neighbours. Imagine if she had been at loggerheads with them previously. What would she have done if she were not on talking terms with her neighbours? Mum, wherever you live or work, please be at peace with all, for you never can tell if and when you will require their help. What's more, you may be the only Christian that your neighbours will ever know.

## Let God Be True

The widow believed the prophet and acted on his words, obeying him completely. It looked illogical, never done before, ridiculous, humanly impossible, yet she believed the anointing upon the life of the prophet and therefore acted on his words or instructions. We are not only to believe in the word of God, our faith must be put into action (2 Chronicles: 20:20). "Trust in the Lord with all thine heart; and lean not unto thine own understanding. In all thy ways acknowledge him, and he shall direct thy paths. Be not wise in thine own eyes: fear the Lord, and depart from evil" (Proverbs 3:5-6).

Partial obedience to God's command is equivalent to complete disobedience. Prayerfully meditate on the words of this hymn written by John H. Sammis:

> *When we walk with the LORD in the light of his ways*
> *What a glory HE sheds on our ways;*
> *When we do HIS good will, HE abides with us still*
> *And to those who will trust and obey,*
>
> *Refrain*
> *Trust an obey, for there's no other way*
> *To be happy in Jesus, but to trust and obey.*
>
> *Not a shadow can rise, not a cloud in the skies,*
> *But His smile quickly drives it away;*
> *Not a doubt or a fear, not a sigh or a tear,*
> *Can abide while we trust and obey.*
>
> *Refrain*
>
> *Not a burden we bear, not a sorrow we share,*

*But our toil He doth richly repay;*
*Not a grief or a loss, not a frown or a cross,*
*But is blessed if we trust and obey.*

*Refrain*

*But we never can prove the delights of His love*
*Until all on the altar we lay;*
*For the favor He shows, for the joy He bestows,*
*Are for them who will trust and obey.*

*Refrain*

*Then in fellowship sweet we will sit at His feet.*
*Or we'll walk by His side in the way.*
*What He says we will do, where He sends we will go;*
*Never fear, only trust and obey.*

*Refrain*

Words: *John H. Sam-mis, 1887.*
Source: *http://cyberhymnal.org*

## CATCH THEM YOUNG

The widow was instructed to go inside with her sons and shut the door. There are two important points to note in this instruction. First, Mum, as you go into action for your breakthrough, you must shut the door of doubt, unbelief, fear, distraction, impossibility, wrong confession etc., behind you. Secondly, get your children involved in the things of God now: don't leave it till later (Please read Proverbs 22:6 and Deuteronomy 6:1-9, especially verses 4-9). When they see the problems, and you all pray together for a solution, believing God, it increases their faith in Jesus Christ when invariably help comes.

A colleague of mine, years back, used to drop her two children (both under 5) at the establishment's Nursery/Day Care Centre, five days a week, from about 0830 hours to late afternoon. Once we got talking, she told me that, though her daughter enjoys Sunday school, she does not take her there every Sunday. When I asked why, she said she prefers the child to personally decide on going to Sunday school when she is of age and can make her own decisions.

Many in society like this lady have got it all wrong. They say it is right to educate a child without the child's choice or approval, but wrong to teach them about the love of God. They also claim it is right to leave the child to choose or reject Christ and His principles; it is right to take children on holidays anywhere at anytime, but wrong to bring them to the home group meetings, Church, prayer meetings, Sunday school, Christian holiday school, Christian children's clubs, etc. Little wonder then, why we have so much social and family problems today.

It is important to allow our children to be involved in praying, reading the Bible, hospitality, visiting the poor, etc. When they are babies, parents should pray for their children and read the Bible to them. Once a child is old enough to ask questions about his food, toy or drink, etc., he is old enough to be prayed with and taught how to pray to God.

A child who is old enough to read the storybooks from the nursery library is old enough to read Children's Bible stories. It is sad to see many children, ages seven and above, from Christian homes who are unable to pray or read the Bible. A write-up from the Daily Bread of October 7, 1994 reads:

"A child may not inherit his or her parent's talents, but he or she will absorb their values. A child takes with him or her, the behaviour and value system modelled by the parents, thus the greatest gift a parent can give you is a worthy example. Whatever you write on the heart of a child, is written indelibly there; each action and word makes an impact you know like a kindness or a beautiful prayer."

## Mind What You Say

The widow involved her sons in the miracle. As the borrowed vessels got filled, she set them aside and asked for another. It got to a time when she asked for another and her son said, "there is not a vessel more", then the oil stopped flowing (v. 6). That negative confession stopped the flow. Negative confessions erase your prayer request thus leaving nothing for God to work upon, someone once explained.

Too many have stopped the flow of God's anointing in their life by their negative confession. We should be moved by faith not by sight and even in the midst of the storm our words should tally with God's words. We should declare His abiding peace and invite His presence into any storm of our life—career, marriage, family or any area whatsoever.

God spoke the world and everything that is in it into existence (Genesis 1:1-31). His words accomplish His purpose; He speaks no careless word (Psalms 12:6; Isaiah 55:10-11). God's words are tested and He is a shield to those who take refuge in Him (2 Samuel 22:31). Every living person is created in God's own image. We as children of God carry His trait; our words like His are powerful so we should watch what we say.

## BE ACCOUNTABLE

The widow upon experiencing the miracle of God's multiplication went back to the prophet and gave him an update. It is always nice to give an update to those whom God uses to point us in the right direction. That certainly encourages the vessel that He had used.

Also, it sometimes leads us to receiving the next

instruction that will perfect our breakthrough. The widow for instance received a third instruction after going to update the prophet: *"...Go sell the oil, and pay thy debt, and live thou and thy children of the rest"* (v. 7). The woman got established in the oil business and saved her son's lives. Mother, as you use that 'except' under the guidance of the Holy Spirit, you will experience your miracle; God's anointing upon you will be multiplied in the process and you will meet the needs of those around you.

God is able to take care of your beginning and end, your past, present and future. Indeed the Lord's blessings make rich and add no sorrow. He alone gives peace and rest. What do you have my sister? As you obediently release it to God with an undivided faith, He will meet your present need and establish your future. What the creditor meant for evil, our God used for this lady's blessings and so He will for you my sister.

## EXERCISE SIX

**Evaluate your life from the unnamed widow's story.**

**A.**

1. Why do bad things happen to good people?


2. What troubles have you suddenly found yourself in?

    a.
    b.
    c.

3. Who have you consulted concerning those problems? When and where did you consult them?


4. When last did you seek for help from the right place and the right person?


**B.**

1. List the debts you or your family members have to settle. Who are your creditors?

    a.

b.

c.

2. Identify what you have that God can use or multiply to bless you.

   a.

   b.

   c.

   d.

   e.

3. Seek God's face for the instructions you need to follow or the Scriptural commands to obey.



4. What doors do you have to shut in order to receive your miracle/blessing?

   ❏ Unbelief

   ❏ Anger

   ❏ Malice

   ❏ Resentment

   ❏ Jealousy

   ❏ Self centeredness

   ❏ Pride

- ❏ Prayerlessness
- ❏ Wickedness/meanness
- ❏ Other (Please specify)

5. How often do you involve your child(ren) in Bible study and fellowship meetings?

   a. Daily
   b. Regularly
   c. Sometimes
   d. Rarely
   e. Never

## C.

1. Is it right to send children to kindergarten for education but not to the Sunday school or Christian holiday clubs?

   - ❏ Right. Explain why:
   - ❏ Wrong. Explain why
   - ❏ Other (Please specify and explain why:

2. When last did you allow your child(ren) to gain first hand experience by involving them in any act of hospitality?

## Chapter 6 - God's Provision—My Part

## Prayer For Help

*Dear FATHER in heaven, I confess that often if not at all times, I cannot but be concerned with bad things happening to good people.*

*I bring before YOU LORD the following areas in which I am struggling (list them please.) FATHER, I ask that YOU by the HOLY HANDS will sort me out.*

*Help me LORD to involve our child(ren) in our challenges especially as we pray together and experience the manifestation of YOUR reply and our victory.*

*Teach and help me that my words may be positive and in line with YOUR words as from now on in JESUS name, I pray and with thanksgiving. Amen.*

CHAPTER SEVEN

# Christmas Is About Willingness

CHRISTMAS IS ABOUT WILLINGNESS and obedience to God "There is a great need on earth," announced God in heaven. Mankind has missed my love and my eternal plans for them. They need to be redeemed from their sins, death and depravity.

As the call went out, only Jesus was willing to pay the price. Betrothed Virgin Mary was God's choice for His mother. Receiving the news from angel Gabriel whilst alone, despite the implication of such on her engagement and life, she was willing to be used as such by the Almighty God. She also willingly obeyed God all through her life.

Joseph, Mary's fiancé obeyed the angel and took Mary as wife willingly, in spite of his knowledge that she was already pregnant, and cared for her all through the nine months of pregnancy. He obeyed the Angel—even after Jesus was born in Bethlehem—in moving the family only to live where God directed him.

The wise men from the East saw in the sky, the great

star, and they willingly travelled several miles to see the newborn King. The shepherds in the fields left their flocks all alone by night in obedience to the angels' annunciation after their departure. Willingly, they went seeking the newborn king to worship Him. Christmas is about willingness and obedience to God. God uses ordinary people to achieve extraordinary missions, men and women of different ages, tribes and nationality—people of different professions and social status world wide.

Beloved, how willing and obedient are you to God this Christmas? God's eternal love and redemption, by the blood of Jesus Christ, can only be received by willing and obedient people. People with childlike faith, who will see themselves as God does, and receive the Child born at Christmas as their Lord and Saviour. For in Christ only is there peace, joy and God's blessing.

God is still in need of obedient and willing people this Christmas, men and women who will be His legs, His mouth, His hands and His ears. Willing and ordinary people of every tribe, status and profession, for the Gospel message of Christmas is still unheard by many. Friend, in willingness and obedience, will you heed that call today?

Copyright © O. Ola-Ojo 25.12.92.

# MARY—MOTHER OF JESUS

Mary, a virgin engaged to Joseph, had an angelic

## CHAPTER 7 - CHRISTMAS IS ABOUT WILLINGNESS

visitation. She was highly favoured by God and blessed amongst women. The angel gave her a word from the Lord about His plans for her and a definite change of her destiny.

## HER STORY

*In the sixth month of Elizabeth's pregnancy, God sent the angel Gabriel to Nazareth, a village in Galilee, to a virgin named Mary. She was engaged to be married to a man named Joseph, a descendant of King David. Gabriel appeared to her and said, "Greetings, favored woman! The Lord is with you!" Confused and disturbed, Mary tried to think what the angel could mean.*

*"Don't be frightened, Mary," the angel told her, "for God has decided to bless you! You will become pregnant and have a son, and you are to name him Jesus. He will be very great and will be called the Son of the Most High. And the Lord God will give him the throne of his ancestor David. And he will reign over Israel forever; his Kingdom will never end!"*

*Mary asked the angel, "But how can I have a baby? I am a virgin." The angel replied, "The Holy Spirit will come upon you, and the power of the Most High will overshadow you. So the baby born to you will be holy, and he will be called the Son of God. What's more, your relative Elizabeth has become pregnant in her old age! People used to say she was barren, but she's already in her sixth month. For nothing is impossible with God."*

*Mary responded, "I am the Lord's servant, and I am willing to accept whatever he wants. May everything you have said come true." And then the angel left. A few days later Mary hurried to the hill country of Judea, to the town where Zechariah lived. She entered the house and greeted Elizabeth. At the sound of Mary's greeting, Elizabeth's child leaped within her, and Elizabeth was filled with the Holy Spirit. Elizabeth gave a glad cry and exclaimed to Mary, "You are blessed by God above all other women, and your child is blessed. What an honor this is, that the mother of my Lord should visit me!*

*When you came in and greeted me, my baby jumped for joy the instant I heard your voice! You are blessed, because you believed that the Lord would do what he said." Mary responded, "Oh, how I praise the Lord. How I rejoice in God my Savior! For he took notice of his lowly servant girl, and now generation after generation will call me blessed. For he, the Mighty One, is holy, and he has done great things for me. His mercy goes on from generation to generation, to all who fear him.*

*His mighty arm does tremendous things! How he scatters the proud and haughty ones! He has taken princes from their thrones and exalted the lowly. He has satisfied the hungry with good things and sent the rich away with empty hands. And how he has helped his servant Israel! He has not forgotten his promise to be merciful.*

*For he promised our ancestors—Abraham and his children— to be merciful to them forever. Mary stayed with Elizabeth about three months and then went back to her own home. Now it was*

## CHAPTER 7 - CHRISTMAS IS ABOUT WILLINGNESS

*time for Elizabeth's baby to be born, and it was a boy. (Luke 1:26-57, NLT)*

## ARE YOU WILLING?

Mary believed and accepted the angel's message and was very willing to drop her personal plans, desires and aspirations for God's own assignment. The punishment for getting pregnant out of wedlock in those days was death by stoning, yet Mary said yes to God. She instantly agreed with His agenda for her life and the world.

Angels are still around us today, ministering the unfailing word of God to His people. How much of God do you know and how willing are you to change your agenda for His own? Should God visit you today with such a request, will your response to Him today and always be, yes?

Mary believed all that she was told and she experienced the fulfillment of them all. She rejoiced at the news of her elderly cousin Elizabeth's miraculous conception and was humble enough to visit her. She did not sit at home in pride even though she knew she was to give birth to the Saviour while Elizabeth carried the forerunner. The sound of Mary's situation caused her cousin's unborn baby to leap for joy in the womb and become spirit-filled. Truly, the words of the wise give life and are soothing.

Mary stayed with Elizabeth for three months, possibly

helping her till after John the Baptist was born. How helpful are you to those in need—the poor, pregnant women, widows or single mothers around you?

## Discretion Protects Destiny

One remarkable thing about Mary is that, although she was happy and believed all that the angel and others told her, she remained humble and discrete. She had Jesus the Saviour of the world in a stable, and placed Him in a manger.

Wise men and shepherds visited the new parents, telling them more about baby Jesus and giving Him gifts. Through it all, Mary and Joseph remained humble and Mary kept the sayings in her heart. When they took baby Jesus to the temple, more prophecies came and, like before, His mother treasured and kept them in her heart (Luke 2:6-39, Matthew 2:1-11).

Many mothers have ruined the destinies of their children by indiscriminately disclosing God's intention for their children to the world. If you are privileged to know about the divine destiny of your child, please protect it by keeping the information to yourself. You should continually intercede and plead the blood of Jesus over the child's destiny, so that nothing will terminate or delay its fulfilment.

If the prophecy is not clear or straightforward, then

spend time before the Lord asking Him for clarity and guidance. Should the prophecy be a bad one, then still take it to the Lord in prayer and, on your knees, ask Him to turn every negative prophecy to a positive one.

Remember God reveals information only to redeem. Write the good prophecy or prophecies down if you can, but most importantly, pray about them and watch out for their fulfilment.

## Intimacy With God

One night, God told Mary and Joseph to relocate to Egypt as King Herod was after their son's life. They risked their lives in order to preserve the life of their newborn son. Satan is still seeking to kill destiny carriers today, especially boys. His trick is the same even though his method might have changed.

Like Joseph and Mary, you need to hear from God concerning the safety and protection of your children. For you to do that, you must have a good relationship with Him. Children are blessings from the Lord and the Bible also says the blessings of the Lord makes rich and adds no sorrow to it (Proverbs 10:22).

Your children therefore, being blessings from God, should in no way prevent you from having a meaningful and prayerful fellowship with Him, neither should they be an excuse for you not to hear Him speak.

## Lead Your Child To God

Mum, please help your child to feel comfortable in Church or fellowship meetings. Attend worship services and meetings together regularly and wisely expose him or her to the ways and words of God?

At age twelve, Jesus went to the temple in Jerusalem with His parents. On the way back to Nazareth, His parents thought He was lost in the crowd and, after three days of active searching, they went back to the temple where they found Him sitting comfortably, discussing with the scholars in the temple. After searching through the crowd without success, Mary and Joseph knew exactly where their son would be.

Freedom of movement does not mean children should not be accountable to their parents concerning their whereabouts. Many children have been maimed or prematurely killed as a result of non-accountability of their movements to their parents. In most cases, such children would have been prevented from going to dangerous places, or quickly sought for, when they did not return home on time.

## Befriend Your Child

Not only does motherhood demand that you spend quality time on your knees, talking to God about your children, you also need to talk to your children too. God's

## CHAPTER 7 - CHRISTMAS IS ABOUT WILLINGNESS

laws concerning teaching and training your children are to be obeyed. Respect your children, but do not be afraid to correct or discipline them. To have long-lasting parental peace here on earth, you need to maintain an open and honest communication with your children.

For instance, you should be close enough to your child—boy or girl—to be able to talk one on one, about a subject like purity before marriage. Bring up your sons and daughters to remain virgins until they are married. Please take time to befriend each one of your children such that they can freely discuss their innermost thoughts and concerns with you.

As a mother, Mary knew who Jesus was and His purpose on earth. I believe that she continuously thought about the angelic visitation and prophecies about Him. She knew her son so well that, at the wedding at Cana of Galilee, she turned to Him when the wine was finished. She knew that whatever instructions Jesus gave would resolve the problem, so she told the servants, "Whatever He tells you to do, do it."

Jesus told the men to fill some jars with water, then He turned the water into wine. This was His first miracle and it introduced Jesus to the disciples (see John 2:1-11).

You may not have experienced an angelic visitation like Mary, but as you take time to prayerfully and carefully watch and be part of your child's growth, you will soon discover many good traits in him or her. For example, you might find your child gravitating towards a particular subject or hobby, or is passionate about certain issues e.g. injustice, sick people, etc., this might give you clues as to what his or her life purpose might be. Prayerfully encourage and support your child's hobby, subject or passion and together positively work through them.

## STIR UP YOUR CHILD

Bathsheba was another mother like Mary. She was very instrumental in her son, Solomon, becoming the successor of King David, just as Prophet Nathan had taught her to say (see 1 kings 1:11-48). Mum, it is necessary for you to know your child's spiritual, emotional and physical state and development. You will find this knowledge helpful in launching your child into his or her destiny.

If the prophecy about your child is clear and positive, then not only should you pray about it, you need to also look for ways to enhance and stir up that child towards God's assigned purpose.

At a wedding many years ago, the groom had words of praise for his mother, telling us how she sat with him in the nights as he prepared for his exams, studying along with him. Can this be said of you Mum, or you are too busy for such? Ben Carson, one of the leading Paediatric Neuro-surgeons in America, had a mother who, though poor and not very well read, set high educational goals for her two sons and supervised them. Both sons today are who they are by God's grace and their mother's help (The full story is in *Think Big* written by Ben Carson himself).

## GIVE ALL THE SUPPORT

Mary followed Jesus all through His ministry giving Him every possible support. It is very easy for a mother to be supportive when her child is pursuing a cause that she as a mother believes in. But your children should be able to count on your solid support even when their choice is totally different from yours; such as a call into the ministry, show business or athletics, as opposed to law or medicine that your family is well known for. Supporting your children is very important. Your support could be emotional, financial, spiritual (such as praying), or physical, just by being present when needed.

God's ways are oftentimes different from ours, but you can have faith that once you have trained your child in the way he or she should go, God will make your child's choice work for good in the end.

Mary's heart must have been pierced as she watched her son, Jesus Christ being arrested, wrongly accused, condemned to die, brutalised, crucified and buried. She probably recalled the prophecy of Simeon when her son was born:

"And Simeon blessed them, and said unto Mary his mother, Behold, this child is set for the fall and rising again of many in Israel; and for a sign which shall be spoken against; (yea, a sword shall pierce through thy own soul also), that the thoughts of many hearts may be revealed" (Luke 2: 34-35).

Today's mother may never have to witness her child actually being crucified, but she experiences the same measure of heart piercing (like Mary), when her child suffers due to congenital malformations or acquired disease.

She watches helplessly as her child suffers pain from injuries sustained in accidents, or dies following accidents due to some other person's carelessness. Her heart is torn when her child is falsely accused and imprisoned in an unjust system, or when her child gets involved in demonic or damaging practices such as robbery, drug addiction, fraud, the occult, or wrong relationships.

Have you noticed that, in most cases, when people are in trouble or in pain, apart from calling on God, they tend to call for their mothers? Mum, is your child calling on you now, but you are too busy to listen or hear the call? You deserve to have a life of your own, but remember that child needs your love and attention too.

Listen to the cry of your child, I mean the cry that comes from the heart, indicating fear, trouble, mistreatment, agony and pain, and also believe what your

## CHAPTER 7 - CHRISTMAS IS ABOUT WILLINGNESS

child is trying to tell you. The mother in the 'Home Alone' series ignored what her younger son was trying to communicate to her regarding being harassed by his older siblings, and that led each time to serious family problems. If the cry of your children is ignored over a period of time, it might come back as misbehaviour of all kinds—bed wetting, joining the wrong group (or gang), complete withdrawal, lack of affection, etc.

No one, but God can feel the pain in a mother's heart when her child is sick or in any kind of trouble. Many times, those agonizing periods cannot be quantified or imagined. My heart and prayers go out to every mother whose heart is being pierced by what her child is going through. Mum, keep praying to the Lord on behalf of that child. Never give up. Our God is full of miracles and your child's case will not be impossible for Him to sort out.

Although Mary could not appeal against the death sentence passed on her innocent son or personally minister to His physical, emotional and spiritual needs, she was physically present with her son all through the ordeal that led to His death. I am sure that nothing could have prepared her for the torture her son was being subjected to, yet she stood by Him through it all.

Mother, please never underestimate the value of the support that you give to your children, especially in times of difficulty, sickness, sorrow, disappointment, rejection, pains, etc. Your support at such times will go a long way, possibly much longer than you can imagine.

CHAPTER 7 - CHRISTMAS IS ABOUT WILLINGNESS

# EXERCISE SEVEN

**Evaluate your life from Mary, the mother of Jesus' story:**

**A.**

1. Suppose God was looking for a God fearing virgin to bless can any of your children be chosen? Why or why not?

2. Mother how often do you have a one on one talk with your child(ren)?

   ❑ Daily
   ❑ Regularly
   ❑ Sometimes
   ❑ Rarely
   ❑ Never

3. List five subjects you discuss most frequently with your child(ren)

   a.
   b.
   c.

d.

e.

4. Are you prepared for an angelic visitation? Why or why not?

5. Knowing that you can only give what you have, how will you rate your personal knowledge of and relationship with God?

   ❏ Very high
   ❏ High
   ❏ Average
   ❏ Low
   ❏ Very low

6. How and where do you learn about God and how to relate with Him?

   ❏ Only from what I hear on Sundays
   ❏ From what others say
   ❏ From what I read in the Bible
   ❏ From my personal time with God in prayers
   ❏ From all of the above
   ❏ Other

## Chapter 7 - Christmas Is About Willingness

7. How willing are you for God to change your agenda for His?

**B.**

1. The words of the wise give life and are soothing. How would you rate your words?

2. Mum and sister will you say you are a blessing or otherwise wherever or whoever you visit?

3. In spite of your greater joy, achievements, blessings, etc. When last did you take time to be with others rejoicing with them however small their accomplishment or blessing is compared to yours?

   When?
   With who?
   What was the occasion?

4. Identify ways you have been disclosing God's intention for your child or children indiscreetly to the world?

**C.**

1. Identify the changes your children have brought into your life and thank God for those changes.

    a.

    b.

    c.

    d.

    e.

2. List the motherhood changes you are struggling with.

    a.

    b.

    c.

    d.

    e.

3. Write down the names of two people you can go to see right away for matured Christian counselling about those struggles. Make contact with them now please.

    a.

    b.

4  Take these changes and your concerns to God in prayers.

**D.**

1. How much have you exposed your children to God, His word and His ways?

2. Do you seldom or regularly take your children to church or fellowship meetings?

   Why?

   Why not?

3. Mum, how comfortable or otherwise does your child feel in those gatherings? What are the reasons for his/her level of comfort or discomfort?

4. Can you rightly predict or do you as a mother know exactly where your child is at any particular time? If not, why not?

**E.**

1. Have you been able to identify God's purpose and the divine destiny of each of your children?

2. How much time do you take in praying over each of your children's destiny?

    - ❑ Daily
    - ❑ Regularly
    - ❑ Often
    - ❑ Sometimes
    - ❑ Rarely
    - ❑ Never

3. In what ways are you being instrumental in launching your child into his or her destiny?

    - ❑ Spending more time with the child in the area of interest
    - ❑ Getting used to the rules of that hobby/subject of that child so you understand that hobby/subject better and be more helpful
    - ❑ Investing in paying for the materials, books, training necessary for child's pursuit in that direction.
    - ❑ Praying with and for the child in that known destiny
    - ❑ Other, please specify

4. How often do you set goals for your children and take time to supervise them in realizing those goals?

## CHAPTER 7 - CHRISTMAS IS ABOUT WILLINGNESS

- ❏ Daily
- ❏ Regularly
- ❏ Sometimes
- ❏ Rarely
- ❏ Never

5. When does your role as a mother end in the life of your children?
   - ❏ When they become 16 or above
   - ❏ When they have left home
   - ❏ When they have gone to higher institution
   - ❏ When they are married
   - ❏ When they become parents themselves
   - ❏ It never ends

**F.**

1. Identify your child(ren)'s major areas of need.
   a.
   b.
   c.
   d.

2. What support can you give your children for each of the needs identified?

3. Identify any reasons why it may be difficult for you to support your child or children at the moment e.g. disobedience to you or family instructions, bringing the family name into disrepute in their choice.

4. Pray over the identified reasons.

5. In what ways is your heart being pierced like Mary's over any of your children?

6. Give your limitations to God in prayers and praise Him: *Be careful for nothing; but in every thing by prayer and supplication with thanksgiving let your requests be made known unto God* (Philippians 4:6).

## Prayer For Help

*Dear FATHER, in the name of JESUS CHRIST, I thank YOU for the privilege of examining my life in the light of the life of Mary the mother of JESUS.*

*Please help me to know and love YOU more and more on daily basis. Help me to be willing to accept YOUR agenda much more than my woman made agenda. Teach me LORD on how to best look after the child(ren) YOU have graciously given to me.*

*Help me FATHER to pray more for our child(ren)'s destiny in YOU, support him/her/them and be a good example to him/her/them. I plead the blood of JESUS over these young people's destiny. I am struggling LORD, over these changes (list them), and I prayerfully seek for matured Christian counselling on ways I could positively overcome these changes/challenges. LORD, I need your help in giving all the support that our child(ren) need as a loving mother.*

*LORD, I come before YOU in the following areas where my heart is being pierced over our child(ren) (please feel free to list them), Help me LORD to be helpful as I launch our child into his/her destiny in JESUS name I pray and with thanksgiving. Amen.*

CHAPTER EIGHT

# A Psalm For Every Mum

A WISE PERSON ONCE said, "Some things only a mum can do, some things only a mum can fix, some things only a mum can know and some things only a mum can understand." This is very true but there are sometimes when mum simply has no answers; everything seems dark and unclear and nothing she does seems to work. Then mum has to look up from her problems to the One who knows all things and can do all things. I have personally found great comfort, hope, strength and assurance in the psalmist's cry in Psalm 121. I believe you will too.

May the Lord enable each one of us to be all that He wants us to be and be a blessing to our families in Jesus name. Amen.

## PSALM 121

*I will lift up my eyes to the hills, from whence comes my help… (v. 1)*

Lord, when I look to the mountains, they seem high up, solid, strong and immoveable. My help however cannot come from the mountains, as they are without life themselves.

**My help comes from the Lord who made heaven and earth... (v. 2)**

Lord in times past, my help has come from you, maker of heaven and earth. Even though you are my Father and Lord by creative and redemptive rights, yet it seems you are so far away from me at the moment as my cries to you for help have not been answered. If you would help me, I know none of your creatures can stand in my way of progress. Right now I need your help against my adversaries and oppressors who to me appear way high up like the mountains.

**He will not suffer my foot to slip. He who keeps me will not slumber. Behold He who keeps Israel and (myself) never slumbers nor sleep... (vv. 3-4)**

Lord, these words express how vulnerable I am without your help. These days, I cannot feel you holding my hands and I fear that I am about to slip. Much as I believe that you do not slumber nor sleep to loose your grip on me, yet I do not feel your hold as before and as a child I am frightened and feel completely alone and abandoned.

**The Lord is my keeper. The Lord is my shade at my right hand. The sun will not smite me by day nor the moon by night... (vv. 5-6)**

Thank you Lord for being my keeper. You have been my protection in times past. Please come and once again be a shade for me from the heat of oppression, injustice, wickedness, poverty and sickness so that they might not smite me in Jesus name.

***The Lord will protect me from all evil. He will keep my soul... (v. 7)***

Please Lord protect me according to your promise from all forms of evil including unbelief which may want to attack my soul at this time of great need and keep my soul from denying you.

***The Lord will guard my going out and my coming in from this time forth and forever... (v. 8)***

Thank you Lord for promising to guard my ways and to be with me forever. As I daily go about my duties and tasks, may I experience your abiding guidance, leadership and protection once more in Jesus name.

Copyright © O. Ola-Ojo 28/01/95

# Opportunity To Become A Christian

*Dear FATHER IN HEAVEN,*

*Thank you for the privilege of reading this book, Indeed I have sinned and come short of YOUR glory. I am grateful to You for sending JESUS CHRIST into this world to come to die on the cross of Calvary for me.*

*I confess with my mouth and I believe in my heart that JESUS Christ paid for my sins, past, present and future. I believe JESUS Christ was buried and on the third day HE rose from the dead. I believe that JESUS Christ will come back again. I accept HIM now to be my LORD, MASTER, SAVIOUR, BROTHER AND FRIEND.*

*I ask in Your mercy for the in-filling of the HOLY SPIRIT so that with HIS help, I can live a victorious life becoming all that YOU have ordained me to be in JESUS name I pray with thanksgiving. Amen.*

If after reading this book you said the above prayers and became a born-again Christian, please take some time to fill the following tear-off slip, and send to the provided address as shown.

The booklet, *Congratulations! You are Born Again,* is for those who have become so through reading this book. It is a booklet that we would like to send to you free. It answers frequently asked questions and sets you on the way to growing in your new-found faith in God.

You are also free to contact any of the organizations listed at the end of the book. I look forward to hearing from you soon.

O. Ola-Ojo

# TEAR OFF SLIP

**Please fill, tear off and mail this slip to the address provided below:**

To receive your free booklet, **Congratulations! You Are Born Again**, simply fill in the form below with all the details requested and send to: **Protokos Publishers, P. O. Box 48424, London SE15 2YL, United Kingdom.**

Title:_____

First name:_____

Surname:_____

Address:_____

_____

Post Code:_____

Email:_____

Phone: *(day)*: _____ *(evening):* _____

Best time to contact you, *(please tick)*:
- ❏ day
- ❏ evening
- ❏ anytime.

Any urgent prayer request(s)? *(Please, use extra sheets if required)*:

_____

_____

_____

_____

_____

TEAR OFF HERE

# BOOKS BY THE AUTHOR

## Provocation, Prayer and Praise
(December 2004)

Complimentary to The Christian and Infertility this book focuses on the story of an infertile woman in the Bible, her provocations, prayer and praise. Whatever makes you incomplete, unfulfilled, less than whom God made you to be, whatever issue of life that the enemy uses to provoke you calls for prayer.

### Key features:
- Some known medical reasons for infertility in the woman
- Why Hannah went to the house of God in spite of her barrenness
- Is it true that the husband is much more than 10 sons to the infertile woman?
- When, where and how to address the source/cause of your provocation
- God's part and your part in that promise
- God is able to meet that humanly impossible need of yours
- A time to celebrate and praise God

### Book Details:
- Paperback: 62 pages
- Language English
- ISBN-10: 1412026903
- ISBN-13: 978-1412026901
- www.protokospublishers.com

*A Reader from London*
*7 Jan 2006 on Amazon.co.uk*
*An excellent easy to read and understand book. The principles shared in this book though primarily are for those trying for a baby could as well be applied to any area of hurt and unfulfilment.*

# The Christian and Infertility

(December 2004)

The Christian and Infertility addresses one of the often neglected needs of Christian couples. It gives an insight into infertility from the biblical and medical perspectives. It is written not only for potential fruitful couples but for pastors, family and friends of these couples. It is written that the Body of Christ might be fully equipped to know and support couples who are facing the challenge of infertility at present.

## Key features:
- Childlessness in the Bible and lessons to learn;
- Some possible physical, medical and environmental causes of infertility;
- Some known spiritual causes of infertility;
- Some of the available treatment options in the UK;
- Choices of fertility treatment;
- Should a Christian professional be involved in fertility treatment?

## Book Details:
- Paperback: 150 pages
- Language English
- ISBN-10: 1412026911
- ISBN-13: 978-1412026918
- www.protokospublishers.com

*A reviewer from Glen Burnie, MD, USA*
*29 Oct 2007 on Amazon.co.uk*
*This book is a great eye-opener for all. It sheds light on infertility from the medical and spiritual angle and gives the reader a balance as I believe every human being is made up of both physical and spiritual part. For balance in life, the two parts must be well fed. One cannot concentrate on the spiritual and neglect the physical. This book which is quite inspiring also reminds us that God has a way of sorting us out... I will recommend it to everybody trusting God for any form of blessing to get one and apply it to their situation. It will definitely bless you and yours.*

# Obstetrics and Gynaecology Ultrasound - A Self-Assessment Guide

June 2005, Churchill Elsevier Publishers, UK

This self-assessment guide is a structured questions and answer book that develops the reader's understanding capability using a simple method in treating related topics. Clinical indications are presented with their corresponding ultrasound findings using appropriate illustrations. A case study approach is followed; presenting the clinical and ethical dilemmas that might arise whilst encouraging students to think. The aim is to reinforce theoretical knowledge within a clinical environment.

**Key features:**
- Over 600 high-resolution ultrasound images
- Covers a wide spectrum of ultrasound curriculum
- Includes a detailed study of fertility
- Aids quick understanding of the subject matter

**Book Details:**
- 468 pages
- ISBN-10: 0443064628
- ISBN-13: 978-0443064623
- Book Dimensions: 24 x 16.8 x 2.6 cm
- www.protokospublishers.com

"...This excellent new book is a study guide... This is an attractive paperback that should be essential reading for trainee obstetric and gynaecological sonographers, whether they are radiographers or radiology or obstetric trainees. It will be of particular value to those preparing for the RCOG/RCR Diploma in Advanced Obstetric Ultrasound and to specialist registrars in obstetrics and gynaecology undertaking special skills modules in fetal medicine, gynaecological ultrasound and infertility..."

**Reviewer: Ann Harper, MD, FRCPI, FRCOG**
Consultant Obstetrician & Gynaecologist,
Royal Jubilee Maternity Service, Belfast, UK
The Obstetrician & Gynaecologist,
www.rcog.org.uk/togonline Book reviews 2006

# Good Mums, Bad Mums
(June 2005)

This is in two parts, the main chapter that can be used for personal or group study, and an accompanying exercise section. The privileged position of a mother is in her being a co-creator with God and bringing forth life (lives). This book compliments one of God's previous revelations to me as contained in the book titled Good Dads, Bad Dads'. Whilst the father could be likened to the pilot of the family plane, the mother can be likened to the force behind the plane –positive or negative. Good mothers are not only co-creators with God, they also do nurture as well as nourish their children physically, emotionally and spiritually.

## Keys features:
- Were all the mothers in the Bible good mothers?
- Lessons from the strengths and weaknesses of seven mothers
- Be encouraged – you are not alone in the assignment of motherhood
- Be motivated in the areas of your strengths
- Learn ways of supporting your husband and children

## Book Details:
- Paperback: 160 pages
- Language: English
- ISBN-10: 1597813486
- ISBN-13: 978-1597813488
- Book Dimensions: 21.4 x 14 x 1.4 cm
- www.protokospublishers.com

# To The Bride With Love
(2007)

Every wise woman preparing to get married knows she will need sound advice, practical tips and solid, heartfelt prayers, of those who have travelled on the road she is about to journey on. In this book, 10 women of different age groups, from different backgrounds and cultures who wedded under various circumstances, individually share their experience with the bride in an intimate, very candid and unforgettable way.

## Keys features:
- To the Bride with Love is the perfect bride's evergreen companion. The content is suitable, relevant and applicable even decades after the wedding day.
- To the Bride with Love is an ideal wedding gift on its own. It can also accompany any other gift (big or small) that you have for the bride but take this hint... the bride will keep thanking you for the book years and years after.

## Book details:
- Paperback: 108 pages
- Language: English
- ISBN-10: 1434302520
- ISBN-13: 978-1434302526
- Book dimensions: 22.4 cm x 15 cm x 1 cm
- www.protokospublishers.com

*One of the best, 19 Jul 2008 Amazon.com*
*Sade Olaoye "clare4good" (UK)*
*This book has really helped my marriage from the onset as I got it as a wedding gift, God bless the giver. It's a must read for relationship improvement and Gods' guidance. I recommend people to get for oneself and also as a great blessing for someone else in love.*

*Review by Oyinlola Odunlami*
*Shallom Bookshop, SE London UK*
*The style of this book reminds me of Francine Rivers, one of the best*

*authors in Christian novels in the USA, whose style is so engrossing that you can't put her books down until you read the end of the story.*

*Nevertheless, the writing style of Oluwakemi is unique, peculiar and distinct to herself. I recommend To the Bride with Love to wives, wives to be, mothers, mentors, youth leaders and workers. Why? The clarity, the focus and the intent of this book is so empowering, encouraging and enlightening that it will definitely mould or re mould a life to achieve its purpose. The truth is, there are very few books that have depth as well as help you to achieve your goals and arrive at your destination. Many books tend to excite you but have no depth; you read and you forget; they do not really change you but this book, To the Bride with Love will definitely leave a word in your spirit and move you to your next level!*

*I believe that this is also a book that pastors will find useful as a manual for marriage counseling, because many books on marriage focus mostly on what you as an individual can gain, your own personal satisfaction while little is said about the sacrifices involved and their importance. As my pastor usually says, it is important to learn from those who have gone ahead, understand why some were successful and others weren't, so that we won't fall where they fell, rather, we would gain more speed, achieve our goals and thereby glorify Christ.*

*So, I invite you not only to get a copy of this life-changing manual for yourself, but also to put it into as many hands as you can afford to, for then the world will definitely benefit and your life will be a blessing to many.*

# Refuge Under His Wings

## Book details:
- Paperback: 100 pages
- Language English
- ISBN-10: 095578980X
- ISBN-13: 978-0955789809
- www.protokospublishers.com

"...an exhaustive analysis of the Book of Ruth in the Bible. The author combines her deep Christian conviction and excellent knowledge of the Holy Scriptures to produce a must read for every Christian, married or single. The book is interspaced with beautifully written prayers, which enables the reader to pause, pray and meditate on the revelations received… The book is also loaded with poetry like 'Thy will be done oh Lord' for those who may be facing an uncertain future or on a cross road of decisions."

**Dr. E.B. Ekpo, MD, FRCP**
Queen Elizabeth Hospital,
Christian Fellowship, Woolwich, London, UK

"… a spiritually sound book… a fine work of thoughtful reading and study… I therefore recommend it to every Christian, married or single…."
**Pat Roach, Senior Pastor**
New Covenant Church, Wandsworth Branch, London, UK

# COMING OUT SOON!!

## Grace or Works?

This book makes you examine a lot of issues in your life, family relationships in particular, that you may have taken for granted or totally ignored. As conveyed right from the rhetorical question posed in the title, Grace or Works, the author stirs you towards asking yourself pertinent questions, thinking through for answers and even getting solutions for unresolved problems.

Have you heard of prodigal wives, husbands, mothers or prodigal fathers? This book identifies and defines them clearly. For anyone experiencing a crises in their relationship with such prodigal family members, this book, which is based on the parable of the "Prodigal son" in Luke 15:11-32 is a one-stop resource material to meet your counselling needs. And just in case you happen to be the prodigal who has caused your relatives much sorrow, there is hope for you in this book.

Interspersed with prayers for you by the author and specific prayers that you can say for yourself, as well as poems to comfort and inspire you, Grace or Works not only asks you questions, it helps you make and maintain the right choices.

### Key features include:
- The younger son's request
- His trip to a far country
- His relationships away from home
- The investment of his inheritance
- His lowest and turning point
- His open repentance and confession to his father
- His big brother's attitude
- Their father's response to both of them

### Book detail(s):
- Paperback
- Language: English
- ISBN: 978-0-9557898-5-4

# USEFUL LINKS & ADDRESSES:

## Aglow International
Website: www.aglow.org

Aglow International is a network of caring women, a faith-building organisation rooted in local groups and international in scope, yet one-on-one in ministry. Their mission is to lead women to Jesus Christ and provide opportunity for Christian women to grow in their faith and minister to others.

## Care for the Family
P. O. Box 488
Cardiff, CF15 7YY
United Kingdom
Tel: (029) 2081 0800
Fax: (029) 2081 4089
Email: mail@cff.org.uk
Website: www.care-for-the-family.org.uk OR www.cff.org.uk

Care for the Family aims to promote strong family life and to help those hurting because of family breakdown. Their heart is to come alongside people in the good times and in the tough times—bringing hope, compassion and some practical, down-to-earth help and encouragement.

## Children Evangelism Ministry, Inc.
P. O. Box 4480
Ilorin, Kwara State, Nigeria
Tel: +234 31 222199
Email: cem562000@yahoo.com

Children Evangelism Ministry Inc., is a Ministry that reaches out with the Gospel to Children before and after birth. The ministry teaches and equips parents, teachers and coordinators of Sunday School and children's clubs. They also have and hold children's clubs, conferences and training seminars.

## Focus on the Family
Tel: 1-800-232-6459
Website: www.family.org

*Focus on the Family* cooperate with the Holy Spirit in disseminating the Gospel of Jesus Christ to as many people as possible, and, specifically, to accomplish that objective by helping to preserve traditional values and the institution of the family.

## Radio Bible Class (RBC) Ministries

P. O. Box 1
Camforth, Lancashire
LA5 9ES
United Kingdom

Among other forms of spreading the Gospel, RBC prints Our Daily Bread, a free daily devotional reading available for residents in the UK and Republic of Ireland.

## The Shepherd's Ministries

5 Brookehowse Road
Bellingham
London
SE6 3TJ
United Kingdom
Tel/Fax: +44 208 698 7222

Email: info@theshepherdsministries.org
Website: www.theshepherdsministries.org

The Shepherd's Ministries helps to bring Children into an experience of worshipping God in truth and in spirit; gives children a world-view based on God's word and mission and helps children to exercise their gifts in local and global missions.

## United Christian Broadcasting UCB

P. O. Box 255, Stoke on Trent, ST4 8YY, United Kingdom
Tel: +44 1782 642 000
Fax: +44 1782 641 121
Email: ucb@ucb.co.uk
Website: www.ucb.co.uk

Among other forms of spreading the Gospel, UCB prints The Word For Today, a free daily devotional reading available for residents in the UK and Republic of Ireland.

www.ingramcontent.com/pod-product-compliance
Lightning Source LLC
Chambersburg PA
CBHW051438290426
44109CB00016B/1603